WELCOME

Since the beginning and through the entirety of military history, armies have relied on mobility. In attack, retreat, repositioning, logistics and supply, mobility is the key to victory. US General George S Patton Jr once said that fixed fortifications were "monuments to the stupidity of man."

While some may argue that point, the prospects for an army to outflank, drive through, bombard and capture enemy strongpoints are enhanced with mobile capabilities. The Vietnam war, which essentially took place from French involvement in its restless Indochina colony in 1946 through to the communist victory in the spring of 1975, presented significant obstacles to mobility. Coastal areas, swamps, dense jungle, rugged mountains, heavy rains and stifling humidity challenged the performance of tanks, armoured fighting vehicles, self-propelled artillery, armoured personnel carriers and supply and logistics vehicles both tracked and wheeled.

Although such conditions existed, a variety of vehicles participated in the Vietnam conflict in service with French, American, South Vietnamese, Australian and other allied forces, as well as the communist North Vietnamese Army and the Viet Cong insurgency sponsored by the Soviet Bloc and the People's Republic of China. While many of the weapons deployed were of World War Two vintage, first fielded a generation earlier, others were new and innovative, on the leading edge of both practical and conceptual warfare.

North Vietnamese Army soldiers atop a Soviet-designed PT-76 light tank in the capital city of Hanoi. *(Bob Tubbs Public Domain via Wikimedia Commons)*

The US M48 Patton tank, for example, was developed with the spectre of war in Europe foremost, but it was used in action for the first time in Vietnam. The Soviet Union supplied the venerable T-34/85 tank along with its PT-76 light tank and other tracked vehicles in a mix of old and new.

The single most innovative tactic tested in the crucible of Vietnam was the US concept of airmobile warfare. For the first time combat

A Bell UH-1 Iroquois or Huey helicopter idles at LZ Rattlesnake during operations in May 1969. *(Archives Branch US Marine Corps History Division)*

troops were airlifted by helicopter – the famed Bell UH-1 Iroquois or 'Huey' – into zones of enemy activity. They were delivered aboard modern 'iron horses' to landing zones (LZ) and were recovered in swift operations that achieved some objectives but led to significant losses among the vulnerable Hueys.

The Vietnam war was not only the swan song for older wheeled and tracked vehicle types, but also a proving ground for new and innovative ground vehicle designs, as well as helicopters in the combat, air ambulance, supply and transport roles. Along with these weapons of war in the air and on the ground, the mettle of military commanders was tested to the extreme.

In this volume, we explore the machines that men drove, rode and flew into battle during that long, protracted conflict in Southeast Asia. Welcome to *Vehicles of the Vietnam War.* ∎

South Vietnamese soldiers prepare an M48 Patton tank for action at the Army of the Republic of Vietnam Armour School in November 1971. *(US Army)*

CONTENTS

Soldiers of the 4th Cavalry Regiment drop a 4.2in mortar round into the weapon's tube from the bed of an M84 mortar carrier in Vietnam. *(US Army)*

A US soldier places a piece of steel along the front of his M113 armoured personnel carrier in the field in Vietnam, 1968. *(US Army)*

An M132 flamethrower tank spouts fire during operations to clear a landing zone in Vietnam, August 1969. *(US Army)*

This Soviet-made SU-100 self-propelled gun is shown during a commemorative event in 2013. *(Creative Commons Vitaly V. Kuzmin via Wikimedia Commons)*

A vintage North Vietnamese T-54/55 adjacent to the entrance to a military museum in Vietnam. *(Creative Commons Zack Knowles via Wikimedia Commons)*

The ZSU-23-4 Shilka was an effective anti-aircraft weapon fielded by the North Vietnamese and Viet Cong. *(US Air Force)*

ISBN: 978 1 83632 024 1
Editor: Mike Haskew
Senior editor, specials: Roger Mortimer
Email: roger.mortimer@keypublishing.com
Cover Design: Steve Donovan
Design: SJmagic DESIGN SERVICES, India
Advertising Sales Manager: Sam Clark
Email: sam.clark@keypublishing.com
Tel: 01780 755131
Advertising Production: Becky Antoniades
Email: Rebecca.antoniades@keypublishing.com

SUBSCRIPTION/MAIL ORDER
Key Publishing Ltd, PO Box 300,
Stamford, Lincs, PE9 1NA
Tel: 01780 480404
Subscriptions email: subs@keypublishing.com
Mail Order email: orders@keypublishing.com

Website: www.keypublishing.com/shop

PUBLISHING
Group CEO and Publisher: Adrian Cox

Published by
Key Publishing Ltd, PO Box 100,
Stamford, Lincs, PE9 1XQ
Tel: 01780 755131 **Website:** www.keypublishing.com

PRINTING
Precision Colour Printing Ltd, Haldane,
Halesfield 1, Telford, Shropshire. TF7 4QQ

DISTRIBUTION
Seymour Distribution Ltd, 2 Poultry
Avenue, London, EC1A 9PU
Enquiries Line: 02074 294000.

M48 PATTON

With the onset of the Cold War, the prospect for land combat between NATO forces and those of the Soviet Union and Warsaw Pact was quite real. Analysis of American tank performance in World War Two simultaneously spurred revisions and improvements to the US armoured force that would serve on the ground in Europe.

The M48 Patton was the third and final iteration of the basic design named for General George S Patton, a legendary commander of armoured formations during World War Two. It was seen as the replacement for the earlier M47, and while it was intended for possible combat in Europe, more than 600 M48s were eventually sent to Vietnam.

Improvements to the M47 were underway by 1951, including the introduction of an egg-shaped, sloping turret cast in a single piece of steel to provide better crew survivability, lighter weight and reduction of an angular profile to diminish the effectiveness of enemy shells. The hull was rounded as well, dispensing with the box-like design of earlier models. Production of the M48 began in 1952 and approximately 12,000 were completed through to 1959 by the Chrysler Corporation, the General Motors Fisher Tank Arsenal and the Ford Motor Company. Enhancements were continually studied and implemented, resulting in at least nine major variants.

The M48A3 was delivered to the US Army in 1963 and reached Vietnam the same year. As the most prevalent model engaged in Southeast Asia, it incorporated the original modifications along with the new driver's hatch and commander's cupola of the M48A1, as well as the improved turret control and transmission of the M48A2. The M48A3 also debuted a new engine, because the earlier 810hp V-12 Continental AVDS-1790-5B gasoline engine had a nasty tendency to catch fire. With the M48A3, the

An M48 Patton of the 1st Battalion, 69th Armored Regiment moves into Viet Cong territory, with soldiers hitching a ride atop the vehicle during Operation Lincoln, March 1966. *(National Archives and Records Administration US Army)*

powerplant was exchanged for the 750hp Continental AVDS-1790-2A diesel engine.

The tank was capable of a top speed of 30mph with road and cross-country ranges of 290 and 180 miles respectively. The new Allison CD-850-6A cross drive transmission was installed, and in 1967 the sub-variant M48A3 Mod B introduced protective boxes covering the taillights, an adapter ring that raised the commander's cupola by five inches and exhaust door louvres.

Primary armament consisted of the 90mm M41 main gun incorporating a T-shaped muzzle brake. In the later M48A5, the main weapon was upgunned to the M68 105mm cannon. Secondary armament across variants consisted of single .30-calibre machine guns and single .50-calibre machine guns that were turret-mounted. The M48 carried a crew of four with the commander seated high and to the right in the turret, with the loader to his left and the gunner below the commander. The driver was located forward and on the left in the hull.

With modifications, the M48 Patton series became the mainstay of the US Army and Marine Corps armoured formations. The first M48s to arrive in Vietnam were assigned to the Marine 1st and 3rd Tank Battalions and subsequently to the reserve 5th Tank Battalion. Army M48s arrived by the late summer of 1965 and entered service attached to the 1st Infantry Division. Each battalion totalled approximately 57 tanks.

Initially, US senior officers approached the use of armour in Vietnam with scepticism, amid concerns relating to performance in the jungles and marshy lowlands of the country as well as the mountains of the interior Central Highlands. In a strange twist, the first Marine M48s arrived in country partly by mistake. When the organic armour of the 3rd Platoon, Company B, 3rd Marine Tank Battalion, came ashore at Da Nang with the Marine Battalion Landing Team, some officers had not realised that the M48 was a component of the formation.

Cavalrymen of B Troop, 1st Squadron, 10th Cavalry Regiment pause with their M48 Patton tank in the Central Highlands of Vietnam, June 1969. *(US Army)*

With a helicopter hovering overhead, M48 tanks of the 1st Battalion, 69th Armored Regiment, assume herringbone defensive positions along a road near Pleiku, April 1, 1966. *(US Army)*

M48 Patton tanks and M548 cargo carriers roll across an open plain as Nui Ba Den Mountain looms in the background, February 8, 1970. *(National Archives and Records Administration)*

This M48 Patton tank is on display today at the Vietnam Military History Museum in Hanoi. *(Creative Commons Ross Huggett via Wikimedia Commons)*

One of the first major deployments of the M48 occurred during Operation Starlite in the summer of 1965, when Marine tanks blasted numerous Viet Cong strongpoints during two days of heavy fighting. In this infantry support role, they reportedly contributed to the success of Starlite, in which 68 communist insurgents were killed and large caches of weapons confiscated. Seven tanks sustained some degree of damage, one of them being permanently put out of action.

Despite the fact that the 57.2-ton M48 was initially held out of jungle fighting, the use of the tanks gradually increased in Vietnam, particularly with the 25th Infantry Division (Tropic Lightning) under the command of General Frederick Weyand, who ordered the M48s of his 3rd Squadron 4th Cavalry, 1st Battalion, 69th Armored, and 1st Battalion, 5th Infantry (Mechanized) into action.

During a significant fight at the village of An Loc in July 1966, Task Force Dragoon, consisting of Troops B and C, 1st Squadron, 4th Cavalry, and Company B, 1st Battalion, 2nd Infantry, trapped a strong Viet Cong force. While the M48s and accompanying M113 armoured personnel carriers fixed the enemy, infantry closed in on both flanks, killing 240 insurgents. Two M113s were lost in the battle.

Although there were few tank vs tank encounters in Vietnam, one memorable fight at the Ben Het forward base, northwest of Kon Tum in the Central Highlands, occurred on March 3, 1969. Soviet-built PT-76 light tanks attacked, one of them detonating a mine and becoming disabled. A second PT-76 scored a direct hit on the turret of an M48, killing two crewmen and wounding two others. Meanwhile, an M48 destroyed another PT-76, as well as a BTR-50 armoured personnel carrier.

Through the course of the Vietnam war, the US supplied M48 tanks to South Vietnamese forces. By 1966, six armoured cavalry squadrons had been formed, and by 1969 this grew to a pair of armoured brigades. The 20th Tank Regiment was constituted in the spring of 1971, equipped with the M48, and the following year two more tank regiments were organised. A total of 343 M48s were delivered to the South Vietnamese through March 1975.

The M48 gave a good account of itself in combat conditions for which it had never been intended. By the end of American military involvement in Vietnam, 123 US-operated M48s had been lost in action or other circumstances. ■

US Marines cover their ears as the 90mm gun of an M48 Patton tank barks at the communist enemy, April 3, 1968. *(National Archives and Records Administration)*

M60 TANK

An M60 tank participating in combat exercises in the mid-1970s. *(US Army)*

The first US-manufactured main battle tank of the Cold War era, the M60 can be considered either a direct descendant of the Patton series or actually as the fourth iteration of the long-serving Patton type.

Although sources differ somewhat as to whether the M60, which was never actually christened a 'Patton series' tank, was deployed in standard combat configuration to Vietnam, it is significant to the period. The M60 was fielded in Germany and other European countries to deter any land aggression by the Soviet or Eastern Bloc militaries, as well as to South Korea in an ongoing American presence to counter the threat of North Korean aggression.

The M60 was derived from existing Patton designs in response to an alarming intelligence report received in 1956 that suggested the Soviet Union was developing a new main battle tank with capabilities beyond that of the familiar T-54/55. Evaluations of the M48 came to the conclusion that the design was quite utilitarian and could accommodate significant upgrades. The improved M60 entered service with the US military in 1960 and became the primary tank of the Army and Marine Corps for the next 20 years. It saw extensive combat with the Israeli Defence Forces during the 1967 Yom Kippur War and later in the Iran-Iraq War of the late 1980s and even Operation Desert Storm in 1991.

Production of the most prominent combat variant, the M60A3, was underway by mid-1970s, while earlier variants such as the M60A1 were being regularly upgraded to new standards. The lengthy M60 production run lasted from 1959 to 1983, and more than 15,000 completed. The last M60 was not retired from active duty until 1997. By that time, its replacement, the M1 Abrams main battle tank, had also undergone numerous upgrades.

The M60 weighed just over 50 tons, and it was this factor that gave American combat commanders pause when considering its potential effectiveness amid the river deltas, swamps and rice paddies of South Vietnam. Nevertheless, the M60 was an impressive combat machine. Its main weapon was the 105mm M68, a license-built version of the British L7A1 cannon, while secondary armament included a Browning M2 .50-calibre machine gun mounted in the commander's cupola and at least one .30-calibre machine gun. At times, a second .30-calibre weapon was mounted coaxially near the loader's

This trio of 60 main battle tanks is shown during field exercises conducted in 1975. *(United States Government)*

An M60 AVLB deploys its bridge during operations in the desert near Camp Coyote, Kuwait. *(US Marine Corps)*

Both the earlier M48 AVLB and M60 AVLB were deployed to Vietnam, the latter remaining in service with the US Army until 2003.

The M728 CEV entered production in 1965 and 312 were produced during the next 22 years, but most of these were built by 1972; some were actually converted from original M60s. Developed as a support weapon for infantry operations, the engineer vehicle provided heavy assault capability with a short-barrelled 165mm M135 gun, a derivative of the British Royal Ordnance L9A1weapon. The M135 is particularly effective in removing barbed wire entanglements, roadblocks, bunkers and other obstructions. If necessary, it is powerful enough to blast walls and buildings that would otherwise provide havens for enemy forces. Secondary armament includes both .30-calibre and .50-calibre machine guns.

The M728 CEV has often been fitted with the Army's M9 Dozer package used for earth-moving and clearing, or the D7 mine plough, a V-shaped implement that lifts and displaces buried land mines to either side as the vehicle advances. A retractable A-frame and winch system was incorporated for vehicle recovery or the removal of obstructions. The first M728 CEV arrived in Vietnam in 1968 and was employed in infantry support, counter ambush and base security operations. Examples of the M728 remain in service today. ■

hatch. A six-round smoke grenade launcher was added on either side of the turret. The 12-cylinder Continental AVDS-1790-2A engine was a proven powerplant that produced 750hp and a top speed of 30mph.

The original M60 turret was similar to that of the M48 Patton, but revisions with the M60A1 and M60A3 introduced a needle-nosed turret that presented a narrower forward exposure to enemy direct fire. A powerful searchlight with white and infrared capabilities was installed in the M60A1, but removed from a large number of M60A3s. The prominent M60A3 upgrade began in 1977 with laser rangefinding equipment and thermal night-vision gear

for the commander, a Hughes VVG-2 laser rangefinder for the gunner and a solid state ballistic computer for improved firing accuracy.

Through nearly 25 years of production, the M60 was produced in at least 15 variants, and the two that were active in Vietnam were the M728 CEV (Combat Engineer Vehicle) and the M60 AVLB (Armored Vehicle Launched Bridge). The M60 AVLBs were modifications to the chassis of the M60 or M60A1 hulls involving the installation of an aluminium scissor bridge or the Military Load Classification 48, 60 or later 70 bridge, sturdy enough to support the weight of an M48 and the later M60 and M1 Abrams tanks.

A prototype of the M728 CEV is shown undergoing tests with the US Army in the early 1960s. *(US Department of the Army)*

In this 1985 photo, an M60 AVLB is shown extending its bridge during winter operations. *(US Department of Defense)*

This M728 Combat Engineer Vehicle is shown with the M9 Dozer assembly and A-frame attachment. *(US Armed Forces Lou Rivera)*

M551 SHERIDAN

The M551 Sheridan was named for Civil War General Phil Sheridan, a hard-driving cavalry commander, and developed to fulfil a need for a reconnaissance airborne assault vehicle. In the end, the M551 proved a disappointment in its airmobile and amphibious roles. It was intended to be deployable by parachute and to ford streams with ease while marrying the speed of a light tank and the firepower of a main battle tank in lethal combination. In the end, the M551 proved a disappointment in its airmobile and amphibious roles, and was the last attempt by the army to field a light tank.

The story of the Sheridan began in 1957 with the establishment of the Army's Ad Hoc Group on Armament for Future Tanks or Similar Combat Vehicles (ARCOVE). The tank's hull was constructed of aluminium alloy, while its turret was steel, and its eventual weight of 16 tons was indeed light compared to other tanks of the day. Its powerplant was the 300hp General Motors 6V53T six-cylinder turbocharged diesel engine, producing a top land speed of 42mph with a range of 373 miles; in water, the Sheridan moved at 4mph. It was served by a crew of four, the driver positioned in the centre of the hull, with the commander in the turret's right rear, the gunner at right front and the loader at left rear.

Considered a potential replacement for both the Army's M41 Walker Bulldog light tank and M56 self-propelled anti-tank vehicle, the M551

This M551 Sheridan of the 25th Infantry Division, nicknamed 'Origin of Sin', pokes its way through thick Vietnamese jungle in 1969. *(US Government)*

continued in development through 1959, with the Cadillac Motor Car Division of General Motors receiving a contract in June 1960 for further pursuit. The tank entered production in April 1965, with 1,700 built through 1970.

Concurrent with the development of the M551 was the execution of a mandate from ARCOVE that tanks should be capable of firing guided missiles by 1965. Work on the intended primary

An M551 Sheridan of the 3rd Squadron, 4th Cavalry Regiment negotiates difficult terrain in Vietnam, December 1969. The mesh at front is a defensive measure against enemy RPGs. *(US Army)*

M551 Sheridans of E Troop, 17th Cavalry, 101st Airborne Division going through exercises at Fort Campbell, Kentucky, in April 1972. *(National Archives and Records Administration)*

Additional sheet armour has been added to the belly of this M551 of the 3rd Squadron, 4th Cavalry Regiment, photographed in 1969. *(US Army)*

Soldiers of A Troop, 1st Squadron, 1st Cavalry Regiment, Americal Division ride atop their M551, nicknamed 'Diana', near Tam Ky, South Vietnam, March 1970. *(US Army)*

weapon of the Sheridan, the MGM-51 Shillelagh guided missile, commenced in June 1959, and the delivery system was determined to be the M81 gun-missile launcher, which was also capable of firing 6in cannon rounds. One immediate concern was the M-81's use of combustible cartridge cases for the 152mm shells rather than conventional shell casings. Initial secondary armament included a single 7.62mm machine gun, with a 12.7mm machine gun added later.

The development of the M551 and its new weapons systems experienced numerous delays, particularly after army inspectors discovered several issues with the tank as it began rolling off the assembly line. Among these were the lack of a serviceable anti-personnel round for the M-81, the alarming ease with which certain ordnance – even larger calibre machine-gun rounds – penetrated its armour, the lack of a proposed bulldozing kit and the absence of night-fighting gear.

At the same time, the Shillelagh brought complications of its own. The guided missile was substantially larger than a conventional shell, so only nine could be carried, along with 20 of the 152mm rounds. Further, the missile's minimum range of 2,400ft meant that it could not be tracked until it had reached that distance from the tank. Combined with the maximum range of the 152mm HEAT (High Explosive Anti-tank) at 2,000ft, the Sheridan had to cope with a dead zone between 2,000-2,400ft. Due to this and the fact that a clash with enemy armour was unlikely, none of the M551s deployed to Vietnam carried the Shillelagh launcher system.

The first batch of 64 Sheridans arrived in Vietnam in 1969. They were assigned to the 3rd Squadron, 4th Cavalry Regiment, 25th Infantry Division, replacing its M48A3 Patton tanks, and the 1st Squadron, 11th Armored Cavalry Regiment, replacing M113 Armored Cavalry Assault Vehicles in its scout sections. Within two years, more than 200 M551s were in country. Subsequent circumstances suggest strongly that the M551 was rushed into deployment before its technical issues were sufficiently addressed.

The Sheridan gained some praise for its firepower, which was highly effective against North Vietnamese and Viet Cong bunkers and strongpoints, while the eventual arrival of the beehive anti-personnel round brought capability to shred enemy infantry concentrations. The tank was manoeuvrable, light and fast. However, it was discovered that these attributes came at a cost.

The M551 proved highly vulnerable to landmines, and both tanks and lives were lost as a result. The ever-present enemy rocket-propelled grenade (RPG) rounds were a real threat as well. The M-81's combustible ammunition sometimes precipitated catastrophic explosions during enemy action, and residue that remained in the gun breech was a constant fire hazard. The significant recoil of the M-81 shook the tank thoroughly, even lifting it off the ground at times, while its short-barrelled muzzle velocity was too low to guarantee penetration of an enemy armoured target should the occasion arise.

The humid and damp climate of Vietnam, along with vegetation that sometimes fouled exhaust and intake equipment, caused the Sheridan's diesel engine to overheat, while water condensation around the turret and radio mount caused failures in fire control and communications. The crew compartment was found to be cramped and stifling, quickly degrading the combat efficiency of the men inside. The army did add some improvements to the Sheridan by 1972, including AN/VVG laser rangefinding equipment, with these tanks identified as the M551A1.

By 1978, the army had phased the Sheridan out of its frontline units, but it did remain in service through the mid-1990s, participating in Operation Just Cause in Panama in 1989 and Operation Desert Storm in 1991, where it fulfilled a reconnaissance role. The Shillelagh guided missile was never fired in anger. ◼

This example of the M551 Sheridan light tank now resides at Yuma Proving Ground, Arizona. *(Creative Commons Mark Holloway via Wikimedia Commons)*

M41 WALKER BULLDOG

ARVN tank crews came to appreciate the M41's firepower and handling characteristics, and its combat record was extensive. During Operation Lam Son 719 in March 1971, the first major armoured clash of the war, 17 M41s engaged the communists. Five M41s and 25 armoured personnel carriers were lost, but the ARVN forces destroyed 22 North Vietnamese T-54 and PT-76 tanks in return. Operation Lam Son ended in a chaotic withdrawal from Laotian territory, with 54 M41s destroyed or captured in the process.

By 1973, about 200 M41s remained in service with ARVN forces, and these were eliminated or surrendered during the successful communist offensive in the spring of 1975. ∎

This M41 Walker Bulldog light tank is on display at the Fort Meade Museum, Maryland. *(Creative Commons Wilson44691 via Wikimedia Commons)*

A South Vietnamese M41 Walker Bulldog light tank engages communist forces in Saigon, 1968. *(US Army)*

Supplied by the United States in relatively large numbers during the Vietnam war, the M41 Walker Bulldog light tank was used exclusively by the South Vietnamese Army (ARVN).

Intended to replace the M24 Chaffee light tank that had seen brief service during World War Two, development of the M41 began in 1944 and, by 1949, the prototype T41E had taken shape surrounding the proposed engine, the 500hp, six-cylinder Continental AOS 895-3 or a comparable Lycoming aircraft engine that could produce a top road speed of 45mph with a range of 140 miles on the road or 60 miles cross country.

Named after General Walton Walker, who had been killed in an automobile accident during the Korean War in 1950, the M41 was intended for close infantry support as an airmobile and rapid deployment light tank. Served by a crew of four, it weighed just under 26 tons and mounted the 3in M32 main gun, considered capable of slugging it out with enemy medium tanks if necessary. Secondary armament included 7.62mm and 12.7mm machine guns.

Although the weight of the new tank rendered its airmobile requirement unachievable, its other attributes were quite positive. Production began in 1951 at Cadillac Division of General Motors plant in Cleveland, Ohio, and nearly 5,500 were built during a three-year run. Although 900 were built by the spring of 1952, it was too late for the M41 to take part in the Korean War, but it became a mainstay of the South Vietnamese armoured forces.

With the escalation of the conflict in the early 1960s, South Vietnam possessed some M24 light tanks previously in service with the French Army, but these were retired as the US Military Assistance Command, Vietnam, was determined to augment the country's armoured capability in size and training along with the introduction of the M41 by late 1964. Between 1965 and 1972, the US supplied 580 M41A3 variants of the original Walker Bulldog to South Vietnam, with engines upgraded for fuel injection.

South Vietnamese tank crewmen operate their M41 Walker Bulldog light tanks during exercises. *(US Army)*

M24 CHAFFEE

The performance of the American Stuart series of light tanks in North Africa and Europe during World War Two revealed some opportunities for improvement in performance. Although mobile and well-suited for reconnaissance, the Stuarts were severely undergunned with 37mm main weapons. By the spring of 1943, a joint venture between the US Army Ordnance Corps and the Cadillac Motor Division of General Motors had been titled Light Tank T24.

The subsequent design incorporated a lightweight 75mm gun adapted from the North American B-25H Mitchell medium bomber, the 16in tracks and torsion bar suspension of the M18 Hellcat tank destroyer and the best attributes of the latest M5 Stuart. The prototype was completed and delivered on October 15, 1943, and a government order for 1,000 Light Tank 24s was issued by the US Army. This was subsequently increased to 5,000 and production began in April 1944. By August 1945, when production ceased, 4,731 tanks had been completed by Cadillac and agricultural machinery manufacturer Massey-Harris. The M24 was named Chaffee in honour of General Adna R Chaffee Jr, known as the father of the US armoured forces.

The M24 weighed just over 20 tons, was powered by the 220hp Twin Cadillac Series 44T24 engine generating a top speed of 35mph. It was serviced by a crew of five, including a commander, gunner, loader, driver and assistant driver/radio operator. In addition to its main M6 75mm gun, the tank was armed with two Browning .30-calibre Model 1919 machine guns and a single Browning M2 .50-calibre machine gun.

The Chaffee saw limited deployment to the European theatre during World War Two, the first of them arriving in France

An M24 Chaffee light tank on display at a museum. The M24 served primarily with French forces in Vietnam. *(Greg Goebel public domain)*

A French M24 Chaffee tank crew is shown during the long siege at Dien Bien Phu in 1954. *(US Army)*

A French Foreign Legionnaire walks ahead of an M24 Chaffee light tank in Vietnam's Red River Delta between Hanoi and Haiphong, 1954. *(National Archives and Records Administration)*

in November 1944. With the outbreak of the Korean War in 1950, the Chaffee was the most readily available American and United Nations armour to send to the aid of the hard-pressed South Korean forces.

The Chaffee engaged a North Korean tank on July 10, 1950, when a company of the 78th Tank Battalion lost two of its number but destroyed the heavier adversary. In Korea, the lack of penetrating power of the M24's 75mm gun against the frontal armour of the Soviet-supplied T-34/85 became readily apparent, and replacements in the form of the medium M4A3E8 'Easy Eight' Sherman medium tank reduced the likelihood that the Chaffee would engage in tank vs tank combat.

Meanwhile, the French Army was supplied with the M24 and fielded the type during its war in Indochina. Ten Chaffee tanks were sent to bolster the French defences at Dien Bien Phu in December 1953. Their crews fought gallantly, firing roughly 15,000 shells during the siege that ended in defeat at the hands of the communist Viet Minh in May 1954.

As US involvement in Vietnam escalated, South Vietnamese forces utilised some Chaffees inherited from the French along with the type's replacement, the M41 Walker Bulldog. ■

The main 76mm gun of an M4A3E8 'Easy Eight' Sherman tank barks during action in the Korean War. *(US Army)*

M4 SHERMAN

The M4 Sherman medium tank is an iconic weapon of World War Two, built in greater numbers than any other armoured fighting vehicle of the period with the exception of the Soviet T-34. More than 50,000 variants of the Sherman were manufactured between 1940 and the mid-1950s.

Rushed into production to counter the emerging medium and heavy tanks of the German armoured forces during World War Two, the Sherman was a tough and resilient tank that simply overwhelmed the enemy on the battlefields of Western Europe. Although its relatively thin armour could not withstand the high velocity 75mm and 88mm rounds of the German PzKpfw. V Panther and PzKpfw. VI Tiger tanks, the Sherman relied on speed, manoeuvrability and sheer weight of numbers to tip the balance on the battlefield. Tank vs tank combat was not its forte, but working tactically in concert, a platoon of five Shermans could overcome a single Tiger.

Named for Union Army General William Tecumseh Sherman of the American Civil War, the M4 medium tank was designed and rushed into production as an improvement to the earlier M3 tank. Built to US Army Ordnance specifications issued in 1940, the Sherman was manufactured at the Chrysler Corporation's Detroit Tank Arsenal.

M4 Sherman tank with its French crew in Vietnam during the First Indochina War, 1950. *(Government of France Gautier Sauteret / Cassowary's Archive)*

This M4 Sherman tank survives as a monument in The Netherlands. *(Creative Commons Joost J. Bakker via Wikimedia Commons)*

Many variants were manufactured, incorporating updates and improving performance. Primary variants included the M4A1, M4A2, M4A3 and M4A4, and the most significant differences among these was the powerplant.

The Sherman made its combat debut at the pivotal battle of El Alamein in October 1942. The British Eighth Army victory over the Axis Afrika Korps was a turning point in World War

In service with the French forces during World War Two, an M4 Sherman tank rolls ashore in Normandy. *(US Army)*

Two, and the appearance of the Sherman in the North African desert contributed to the triumph. Afterward, the Sherman was fielded in Italy and an amphibious (Duplex Drive) variant struggled to come ashore on D-Day in Normandy. The Sherman was in the vanguard of Allied troops fighting through the hedgerow country of France, into the Netherlands and across the German frontier. A relative few were sent to the Soviet Union under the Lend-Lease programme.

Some later models of the M4 were equipped with a high velocity 76mm main gun, replacing the original 75mm M3 L/40 that had proved ineffective against German armour. British engineers upgunned the Sherman turret with the Ordnance QF 17-pounder gun and dubbed the more powerful M4 the 'Firefly'; this variant proved a formidable tank vs tank opponent. Incidentally, the M4 was the most numerous tank in service with the British Army during World War Two, and these were provided through Lend-Lease as well.

Indicative of the M4 Sherman variants, the M4A4 entered production in the summer of 1942 and 7,499 units were completed through November 1943. The M4A4 hull was lengthened from the original to accommodate its Chrysler A57 30-cylinder multibank gasoline engine that produced a top speed of 29mph with a road range of 100 miles and cross-country range of 60 miles. The M4A4 weighed nearly 35 tons and carried a crew of five, including commander, driver, gunner, loader and co-driver/hull gunner. The Sherman stood more than nine feet high, and its distinctive silhouette was a disadvantage in combat as the enemy could easily target the tank on open ground. Secondary armament included a pair of .30-calibre machine guns and a turret-mounted .50-calibre machine gun.

Although the Sherman was at a distinct disadvantage against German tanks and earned the derogatory nicknames of 'Ronson', alluding

to a popular cigarette lighter of the day, and 'Tommy Cooker' due to its tendency to brew up when hit by large-calibre shells, the tank was also praised for its speed and manoeuvrability in difficult terrain and its ease of maintenance in the field. During the course of World War Two, the Sherman was modified for special tasks and its chassis provided mobility for a number of specialised vehicles, including mine-clearing flail tanks, flamethrower mounts, ammunition carriers, bulldozers, recovery vehicles and more.

The Sherman tank was deployed during the Korean War in limited numbers as its replacement, the M24 Chaffee, became available in greater quantity.

Meanwhile, the French Army utilised the M4 against its communist Viet Minh adversaries during the Indochina conflict. On December 18, 1950, the French Far East Expeditionary Corps authorised the formation of the Far East Colonial Armoured Regiment (RBCEO) with a complement of 899 troops and 59 Sherman tanks. Presumably many

of these were the M4A3E8 or 'Easy Eight', which incorporated a horizontal volute suspension system, improved armour protection and the 76mm main weapon.

The French believed that they might well encounter a Soviet T-34/85 medium tank, arguably the best weapon of its kind fielded during World War Two and supplied to the Viet Minh through either their Soviet or communist Chinese benefactors. Therefore, they received the M4 with some relief. The Sherman was involved in numerous ground support encounters against communist guerrillas, such as the fighting at Hoa Binh from November 1951 to February 1952. From December 10-14, French counterattacks attempted to check Viet Minh ground advances. When the 5th Colonial Parachute Battalion moved forward, its heaviest support was in the form of five M4 Sherman tanks. The most extensive use of the Sherman in Vietnam occurred from 1950 through 1952, as it was gradually supplanted by the Chaffee.

Nevertheless, the M4 remained in service through the French experience. Further, its service life was extended with the armed forces of many nations into the 1970s. ■

The crew of an M4A3E8 'Easy Eight' Sherman tank pauses during fighting in Korea. *(US Army)*

French airborne troops in the field in 1954. Soldiers like these were supported by M4 Sherman tanks in combat against the Viet Minh. *(Personal Collection Davric Public Domain)*

CENTURION

One of the longest-serving tank designs in modern military history, the Centurion was developed during World War Two in response to the battlefield experience of Allied tank crews against the medium and heavy tanks of the German armed forces. The Centurion was conceived by the British Department of Tank Design between 1943 and 1945, and production was undertaken by Leyland, Royal Ordnance Factories and Vickers near the end of the conflict.

The Centurion did not arrive in the field in time to participate in World War Two, reaching the European continent in May 1945, just days

One of the first Centurions of C Squadron, 1st Armoured Regiment, arrives in Vietnam, rolling off a US landing craft. (Creative Commons Australian War Memorial via Wikimedia Commons)

A Centurion tank of C Squadron, 1st Armoured Regiment, negotiates thick jungle terrain in South Vietnam, 1968. (Creative Commons Australian War Memorial via Wikimedia Commons)

after the war came to a close. However, it was manufactured in substantial numbers, with 4,423 completed through a 17-year production run that ended in 1962. One of the best tank designs of the post-war era, the Centurion remained in service with some military organisations into the 1990s.

The Centurion A41 was the initial response to the War Ministry's 1943 requirement for a tank that could slug it out with German armour. The original of more than a dozen variants or Marks, it weighed a hefty 57 tons and was powered by the 650hp Rolls-Royce Meteor petrol engine producing a top speed of 21mph and an operational range of 280 miles. The earliest armament was the proven QF 17-pounder gun, which was later followed by the 20-pounder and the 105mm L7A2. Secondary armament consisted of a single Browning .30-calibre machine gun. The Centurion A41 armour reached a thickness of six inches (150mm), and through its half-century of service the tank's armour protection was augmented. A crew of four included the commander situated on the right side of the turret, both gunner and loader in turret positions and the driver seated forward and to the right in the hull.

While the Centurion's longevity is attributable to a sound basic design that could accommodate modifications with relative ease, the tank's substantial drawbacks were its mediocre speed, limited range and average cross-country mobility. Even so, its qualites outweighed the drawbacks. The tank first experienced combat with United Nations forces during the Korean War. Centurions of the 8th King's Royal Irish Hussars fought North Korean forces at the battle of the Imjin River, covering the retreat of the heavily outnumbered 29th Infantry Brigade and earning high praise. US General John O'Daniel, commander of I Corps, commented: "The 8th Hussars have evolved a new type of tank warfare. They taught us that anywhere a tank can go is tank country – even the tops of mountains."

Over the years, the Centurion became a mainstay of the armoured forces of many nations. By the early 1970s, the Israeli Defence Forces were the top user, with 1,100 in service. One of the most famous variants of the Centurion was the Israeli Sho't that fought Soviet-built T-54/55 and T-62 tanks of the Syrian Army during the 1973 Yom Kippur War.

In Vietnam, the Centurion served with Australian troops following a commitment

Crewmen of an Australian Centurion tank talk with soldiers during operations in Vietnam, July 1968. (Government of Australia)

Centurion tanks of A Squadron, 1st Armoured Regiment, advance along a dirt road in Vietnam, January 1970. *(Creative Commons Peter Anthony Ward via Wikimedia Commons)*

to increase the country's participation in the war in Southeast Asia. In early 1966, the Australian government announced its intent to raise its forces to brigade strength. The 1st Battalion, Royal Australian Regiment, which had served as a third battalion of the US 173rd Airborne Brigade, was to be withdrawn. In its place the 4,500-man 1st Australian Task Force (ATF) brought soldiers from Australia and New Zealand in country along with organic artillery, aircraft and tanks.

Within months of initial deployment the Centurion was committed to the battlefield. In February 1968, the first 15 were loaded aboard a freighter bound for South Vietnam. These arrived at Vung Tau on February 24 and were transported inland. This squadron formed of two troops of four tanks each, along with headquarters tanks, bulldozers and bridgelayers. Further deliveries raised the total of Centurions in country to 26 by August.

During Operation Pinnaroo on March 8, 1968, a dozer Centurion fired the tank's first shot in anger, a 20-pounder round. Amid five weeks of operations, the Centurions employed direct fire to reduce Viet Cong strongpoints in the Long Hai Hills. Some external armour plating was discarded during the traverse of jungle terrain due to clogging and tangling. As a result, extensions from the tanks' hulls, including lights, were sometimes torn from the chassis.

After the military failure of the communist Tet Offensive in early 1968, the Centurions were also involved in repelling a second enemy offensive called 'Little Tet'. The enemy reached the capital of Saigon in May, but was finally repulsed. During the retreat, the ATF intercepted the communists and engaged in pitched fighting as Centurions covered cross-country distances up to 75 miles in support.

Toward the end of May 1968, the tanks and infantry of the ATF participated in their first

combined operation since fighting the Japanese on the island of Bougainville in World War Two. Infantrymen of D Company, 1st Royal Australian Regiment, and tanks of 1st Troop, C Squadron, conducted a reconnaissance in force. The infantry identified targets with rounds from M79 grenade launchers and the Centurions then rolled forward, two or three abreast, blasting communist bunkers with their main guns or simply crushing them beneath their tracks.

With the conclusion of Australian participation in the Vietnam War a total of 58 Centurions had been deployed. Forty-two of these received some degree of battle damage, with six totally destroyed. Only two Centurion crewmen were killed in action in Vietnam. ■

A Centurion tank crew pauses in Bien Hoa Province to talk to Vietnamese villagers in May 1968. *(Creative Commons Errington, William Alexander (Bill) via Wikimedia Commons)*

Israeli Sho't variants of the Centurion in 1969. *(National Library of Israel)*

Soldiers of the US Army's 77th Infantry Division trudge past M8 howitzers parked along a roadside, Okinawa 1945. *(Signal Corps Archive)*

M8 HOWITZER

Based on the chassis of the M5 Stuart light tank and its pairing with the M2/M3 75mm howitzer, the Howitzer Motor Carriage M8 was produced by the Cadillac Motor Division of General Motors from September 1942 though January 1944, with a total of 1,778 manufactured. In November 1944, the US Army Ordnance Department nicknamed the M8 the 'General Scott' or simply 'Scott' in honour of General Winfield Scott of the American Civil War era.

The M8 was deployed first with Allied troops in the Italian campaign during World War Two and participated in the drive on Rome. Later it was used as an infantry support weapon in the advance across France and into Germany by the Western Allies. In the Pacific theatre, the M8 mounted a heavier weapon than any Japanese tracked vehicle and was effective against bunkers and enemy troop concentrations. However, by 1944, heavier 105mm self-propelled guns were mounted on the versatile chassis of the M4 Sherman medium tank, supplanting the M8 in its primary role. During World War Two, the M8 was used by both the US Army and Marine Corps, the Free French forces and Yugoslav partisans fighting in the Balkans. The Philippine armed forces inherited some examples of the M8 from American units based there.

After World War Two, the M8 was utilised by French forces in the early years of the war in Southeast Asia, sometimes referred to as the First Indochina War. The French also provided some serviceable M8s to the Vietnamese national army fighting against the communist Viet Minh. After the French withdrawal from Southeast Asia, the South Vietnamese Army fielded a few M8s as well.

After months of unsatisfactory trials with the chassis of both the M3 and M5 Stuart light tanks, the T-47 project produced the most workable self-propelled artillery design with a manually rotated, open topped turret and crew of four.

The commander was positioned to operate the .50-calibre Browning machine gun against low-flying aircraft in the event of enemy action, while the driver and assistant driver/loader were seated forward in the hull, while the gunner was positioned in the turret to the right of the howitzer.

The M8 was powered by the Twin Cadillac Series 42 inline six-cylinder petrol engine, which produced 220hp, a top road speed of 36mph and a range of 100 miles. Its armour protection was relatively thin from .75 inches to 1.75 inches, making the weapon quite vulnerable to even medium calibre shells. The tank weighed 15.7 tons and carried 45 rounds of 75mm ammunition. These were stowed in the rear of the fighting compartment and a hull sponson to the left rear. Six rounds were readily available, situated between the driver and assistant driver/loader positions. ■

This M8 Scott self-propelled howitzer is on display at the Musée des Blindés in Saumur, France. *(Creative Commons Fat yankey via Wikimedia Commons)*

M8 Scott self-propelled howitzer blown over by communist Viet Minh fire during the June 1954 battle of Mang Yang Pass. *(Vietnam People's Army)*

M106 MORTAR CARRIER

Soldiers of B Troop, 3rd Squadron, 4th US Cavalry, operate an M106 mortar carrier in Vietnam on January 8, 1967. *(US Army)*

An M125 with an 81mm mortar in service with Australian troops crosses a bridge during Operation Matilda in Vietnam, February 1970. *(Creative Commons Australian War Memorial via Wikimedia Commons)*

From the inception of the famed M113 armoured personnel carrier in the 1950s, it was expected that numerous variants would arise, giving the vehicle a versatility not only in troop and supply transport, but also in providing indirect fire support to infantry units engaged with the enemy.

The M106 mortar carrier was one of the best-known of these variants. Utilising the tracked chassis of the M113, the M106 featured a mounted M30 107mm mortar in a mobile platform. The M107 could be fired from within the vehicle or set up separately by assembling the baseplate and bipod, which were carried on the side of the vehicle. The M125, another variant of the M113, mounted an 81mm mortar in similar fashion.

Manufactured by FMC Corporation, the M106 was constructed of aluminium, with thickness ranging from 1.18in to 1.77in, which made the vehicle susceptible to enemy large-calibre weapons, in particular the rocket-propelled grenades that were made available in quantity to North Vietnamese troops and Viet Cong guerrillas by their Soviet benefactors.

The M106 was powered by the 215hp, eight-cylinder Chrysler 75M petrol engine delivering a top speed of 39mph and a road range of 211 miles. The M106A1 variant was powered by a 210hp, multi-cylinder Detroit Diesel 6V53T engine that delivered similar performance. TheM106A2 brought an improved suspension and engine cooling capacity that were features of the M113A2, along with enhanced elevation capability for the M30 mortar, increasing its effectiveness with full range while the vehicle was on flat ground. The M106 entered service in 1961 and remained in production for more than a decade, with 2,621 completed, comprising 862 in the standard M106, 1,409 in the M106A1 and 350 in the M106A2.

Like the M113, the M106 was highly visible in the field with its height of more than seven feet, high flanks and distinctive silhouette. The vehicle was fully tracked with an idler to the rear, drive sprocket in the front and five road wheels. It weighed nearly 13 tons and was nine feet wide.

A crew of six serviced the M113, operating the mortar from inside the vehicle via a large circular split hatch atop the crew compartment. The mortar was mounted on an internal turntable and fired through the open hatch unless circumstances dictated that the crew dismount and set up the weapon externally. The vehicle carried up to 93 rounds of 4.2in ammunition, although the capacity of the M106A1 was reduced slightly to 88 rounds. The M125 carried 114 rounds of 81mm ammunition. Secondary armament included a pintle-mounted .50-calibre Browning M2 heavy machine gun.

The modified M106 remains in service with numerous countries, with some extant examples upgunned to carry an 120mm mortar. ∎

Troops of Company D, 16th Armor, 173rd Airborne Brigade, fire their 4.2in mortars from the M106 during Operation Toledo in Vietnam. *(Creative Commons WWW3ii via Wikimedia Commons)*

M53/M55
SELF-PROPELLED HOWITZER

The M53 and M55 self-propelled howitzers represented steps in the progression of US Army mobile artillery doctrine that emerged during World War Two, when such vehicles as the M7 105mm howitzer carriage, nicknamed 'Priest' by its British users, came to the forefront.

By 1950, the next generation of self-propelled artillery was in full swing with the concurrent T97 and T108 projects, which would mature into the M53 155mm and M55 203mm mobile platforms. The Pacific Car & Foundry Company produced both models, with the first production M53 vehicle rolling off the assembly line in August 1952. Production of the M53 continued until the spring of 1955, while M55 production continued for another year. The two vehicles shared common design and other attributes, but with the conclusion of M53 production some existing examples were upgunned to the 8-inch M55, with 550 in service by 1956.

The self-propelled howitzers retained the chassis of the M46/47 Patton tank but re-engineered the powerplant to a forward position along with the transmission. This change brought frontal protection from indirect fire to the six-man crew, with the commander, driver, gunner and ammunition handlers situated inside an enclosed, box-like turret.

With these mobile howitzers intended to provide heavy, long-range firepower in a capable cross-country configuration, their powerplant was the 810hp Continental AV-1790-5B, 12-cylinder petrol engine with a

M53 and M55 self-propelled howitzers during firing exercises. *(US Department of Defense)*

top speed of 30-35mph (the heavier M55 was a bit slower) and range of about 150 miles. The driver initially used a tiller or 'wobble stick' arrangement and, as improvements to the M46/47 occurred, they were undertaken with the howitzers as well, including an upgraded Continental AV-1790-7B engine, a new transmission and a steering wheel for the driver.

The turret was constructed of welded homogenous steel with a maximum thickness of nearly one inch, while the roof was flat with sloping sides, and both top and rear hatches were opened for the 155mm gun, to ease servicing in combat and reduce recoil since no mechanism for that purpose was built into the gun itself. On the M53, the 155mm M46 howitzer, nicknamed 'Long Tom', was emplaced on the M86 mounting and provided with 20 rounds. The 8-inch M47 howitzer turret could accommodate 10 rounds of ammunition. Secondary armament for both the M53 and M55 consisted of a single .50-calibre Browning M2 machine gun installed on a rail that circled the commander's cupola on the right side of the roof. The respective range of the big howitzers was 18,600 yards for the 203mm and 27,340 yards for the 155mm. At such distances, the weapon was usually situated a safe distance from retaliatory fire. Such was the case with the M55 in Vietnam until longer-range

Soviet-made self-propelled guns were made available to the North Vietnamese Army.

While the US Army proceeded with conversion of its M53s to M55s, the Marine Corps retained its M53s. The M53 was never used in Korea, but after the conversion programme of the mid-1950s, the M55 was sent to Vietnam, serving until replaced by the M110. ■

This M55 self-propelled 8in howitzer is on display at Aberdeen Proving Ground, Maryland. *(Creative Commons Mark Pellegrini via Wikimedia Commons)*

In this 1968 photo, an M55 8in self-propelled howitzer fires a round near the US base at Da Nang, South Vietnam. *(US Department of Defense)*

M107
SELF-PROPELLED GUN

While the US Army and Marine Corps endorsed the production of the M53 and M55 turreted self-propelled howitzers, a requirement for a lighter, airmobile self-propelled gun emerged in the 1950s.

The Pacific Car & Foundry Company responded with the 175mm T235 self-propelled gun and the concurrent T236 203mm guns. The T235 entered service with the US Army in 1962 and the M110 a year later. When the company received contracts for both, the development of a common chassis was pursued. With the same drivetrain as the M578 light recovery vehicle, the chassis included five road wheels with torsion bar suspension. The M107 was also manufactured by FMC Corporation and Bowen-McLaughlin-York. Only 524 M107s were completed by the end of production in 1980.

The power plant was the 405hp, eight-cylinder General Motors 8V71T supercharged diesel engine, producing a top speed of 50mph and range of 450 miles. The engine was equipped with a hydraulic pump that traversed the turret, while a back-up manual crank was also installed.

Only minimal protection was provided for the crew, which included 13 personnel, while space for only five was available on the vehicle itself. Armour consisted of only a half-inch of aluminium, which was only capable of deflecting small-arms fire. Kevlar shields were made available, but these were awkward in the field and used sparingly.

The 175mm M113 or M113A1 main gun had a range of nearly 25 miles depending on whether the long-barrelled 60-calibre or short-barrelled 30-calibre was in use. Its rate of fire was approximately two rounds per minute. Two ready rounds were carried in trays aboard the open mount, while additional rounds were available via the accompanying M548 ammunition transporter. Hydraulic spades allowed the M107 to quickly dig itself into a secure firing position to diminish recoil.

The M107 served with distinction in Vietnam, its relatively light weight of roughly 31 tons allowing it to fire and displace, avoiding enemy counter-battery fire. The 'shoot and scoot' tactic served US Army and Marine infantry unit well, while the long range of the weapon made it effective over substantial distances. Its overall performance was superior to Soviet-built self-propelled weapons made available to communist forces as the war progressed. Its ability to degrade North Vietnamese and Viet Cong supply transport, battlefield strongpoints and command and control centres gave US and South Vietnamese troops a distinct advantage. Its contribution to the defence of the forward base at Khe Sanh in early 1968 was a key factor in lifting the lengthy siege.

Still, there were drawbacks with the M107, including the requirement for an ammunition carrier, the 175mm gun's degrading accuracy as range increased and the gun barrels requiring frequent changes due to fatigue, particularly with the early short-barrelled version. A number of M107s were captured by communist forces during the war, particularly after the US exit from Southeast Asia, and these were turned against the South Vietnamese during the decisive offensive that ended the war in April 1975.

Although retired from the US military in 1978, the M107 saw extensive service with other countries, including Israeli forces in various Middle East conflicts. Some examples remain in service today. ∎

An M107 175mm round used in a distant US fire support base in Vietnam. *(US Government)*

An M107 self-propelled gun in service with the Dutch military. *(Creative Commons Leger Film- en Fotodienst (LFFD) via Wikimedia Commons)*

An M107 self-propelled howitzer crew fires its 175mm gun at a distant target in Vietnam, 1968. *(US Army Heritage and Education Center)*

M108 SELF-PROPELLED HOWITZER

The short-barrelled 105mm howitzer is prominent in this photo of an M108 from 1961. *(US Government)*

During the early years of the Cold War, the US military embarked on a programme of mobile artillery development that involved self-propelled guns and howitzers of various calibres utilising common chassis and other components wherever possible to minimise design time, development cost and manufacturing expense.

One of the earliest self-propelled artillery vehicles adopted was the 105mm M108 howitzer, which became serviceable in the 1950s. The M108 was developed concurrently with its heavier counterpart, the 155mm M109 howitzer, and the two platforms shared much of their composition.

The M108 weighed 21 tons and stood nearly 11ft high. Its 425hp, eight-cylinder Detroit Diesel 8V-71T turbocharged engine produced a top speed of 35mph and range of nearly 224 miles. Its armour protection reached 1.25 inches in thickness. The crew of five included the commander, driver, gunner and two ammunition handlers, each of them located within the turret except for the driver, whose position was forward in the hull.

The M108 carried 87 rounds of 105mm ammunition for the M103 howitzer, which was situated in the rotating turret with 360° traverse. The rate of fire was four rounds per minute and the effective range stretched beyond seven miles. Secondary armament included a .50-calibre Browning M2 heavy machine gun mounted adjacent to an upper turret hatch for defence against aircraft, light armoured vehicles and enemy infantry, while small arms such as the M-14 rifle were available to crewmen for close combat if needed. Hatches were installed in

With spent 105mm shell casings visible at lower right, an M108 in Vietnam. *(US Government)*

the rear of the turret and hull to allow easy replenishment of ammunition and stores, as well as to dispense with empty shell casings.

In Vietnam, the M108 was often deployed to forward operating bases and regularly utilised in direct fire support of infantry and armoured units in the field. The platform reached Southeast Asia with the 3rd Battalion, 6th Field Artillery Regiment, located at Camp Saint

This M108 self-propelled howitzer is on display at a museum in Taiwan. *(Creative Commons 玄史生 via Wikimedia Commons)*

Barbara outside the city of Pleiku on June 17, 1966. A component of the 52nd Artillery Group, the 3rd Battalion and its M108s participated in ten campaigns in the Central Highlands of Vietnam before its withdrawal in April 1970.

The 1st Battalion, 40th Field Artillery Regiment, was based at Dong Ha Combat Base and operated the same 18 original M108s from October 1966 through three years in country. The M108s of the 1st Battalion fired more than a million 105mm rounds and its unit history notes: "The 1-40th FA was located at Camp Carroll in the vicinity of Dong Ha on Highway 9 just west of Highway 1, 10 miles south of the demilitarised zone (DMZ) in Vietnam. 1-40th FA was among the first US Army field artillery units in I Corps' area of operation and was the first artillery unit to fire into North Vietnam. The battalion operated in Quang Tri City, Ca Lu, Cam Lo, the Rockpile and north of Dong Ha."

The M108 was active throughout US involvement in Vietnam, but was phased out by 1975 in favour of the heavier M-109. Usage by other militaries peaked in the 1980s, but some examples remain in service. ■

M109 PALADIN SELF-PROPELLED HOWITZER

An early variant of the M109 'Paladin' in service with the Dutch Army. *(Creative Commons Leger Film- en Fotodienst (LFFD) via Wikimedia Commons)*

An M109 155mm howitzer halts along a dirt road in Vietnam. *(US Army)*

I n keeping with the US Army initiative to provide ground forces with mobile artillery support while utilising existing components as much as possible, the M109 Paladin self-propelled howitzer was developed in the early 1960s and deployed to Vietnam. It has since become an iconic symbol of Western firepower in the ground support role.

The Ground Systems Division of United Defense LP, now a subsidiary of BAE Systems Land and Armaments, brought forward the blueprint for the M109 as a replacement for the earlier M44 self-propelled howitzer. The M109, nicknamed 'Paladin', shared common construction with the lighter 105mm M108 and the M113 armoured personnel carrier. The first production model was accepted into service with the US Army and Marine Corps in 1963 and, since then, more than 7,700 have been built by numerous manufacturers in many variants.

With its 23-calibre M126 155mm howitzer, the M109 was conceived as the medium variant for the army's mobile artillery component. With the M109A2 introduced in 1973, the main weapon was upgunned to the 39-calibre M185 155mm howitzer; more recent versions mount the M284 155mm howitzer. The early 155mm howitzer had a range of 11 miles, a rate of fire of four rounds per minute and 28 rounds were usually carried aboard due to their size and the requirement for separate propellant charges. Secondary armament consisted of a single Browning .50-calibre M2HB machine gun.

The original M109 powerplant was the 345hp, eight-cylinder General Motors 8V71T diesel engine, yielding a top speed of 35mph and an operational range of 216 miles. The crew of six included a commander, driver, gunner and up to three ammunition handlers, although later automation of some functions reduced the crew to four. Like the M113, the armour protection of the M109 consisted of rolled aluminium alloy welded together with thickness of roughly 1.25in. The driver was located in the front left of the hull, while other crew were seated in

An M109A6 fires its 155mm howitzer at night. *(US Air Force)*

the enclosed turret. Both hull and turret were rather box-like in shape, but the forward section of the turret was distinctively rounded. Fully loaded, the M109 weighed 27.5 tons. It stood nearly 11ft tall and was nearly 10½ft wide.

The M109 was deployed to South Vietnam in 1966, with 200 vehicles initially arriving in country. Mechanical problems plagued the vehicles during their first year in operation, to the extent that engineers were sent from the US and many were recalled for significant repairs that resulted in the improved M109A1.

The history of the 4th Battalion, 11th Marine Regiment, 1st Marine Division, relates that the unit's M109s were regularly firing into North Vietnam from positions south of the demilitarised zone (DMZ) by the summer of 1967. Counter-battery fire was a primary function of the 'Paladin', and its armour protection served the crew well when exchanges with communist artillery occurred. The 4th Battalion further deployed its M109s during the battle for the provincial capital city of Hue during the Tet Offensive of 1968, providing fire support to Marine infantry engaged in urban fighting with Viet Cong insurgents.

The Army's 1st Battalion, 27th Field Artillery Regiment trained for three months at Fort Sill, Oklahoma, before shipping out to South Vietnam in February 1967. Six M109s of Bravo Battery were located at the Tay Ninh base camp, where they fired in support of infantry operations against the communists in the Cu Chi area. An American communications station atop an extinct volcano called Nui Ba Den or Black Virgin Mountain by US soldiers, was constantly harassed by Viet Cong insurgents and could only be resupplied by air. The M109s focused suppressing fire on the enemy when activity was noted, sometimes loosing a heavy volume of fire and preventing the position from being overrun. During the 1968 Tet Offensive, the battery was ordered from its post at a rubber plantation at Dau Tieng back to Tay Ninh. However, a second battery's M109s were not mission-capable and those that were running were required to tow the others back to their original base.

The size and weight of the M109 somewhat restricted its movement to improved roadways

An M109 of the 11th Marine Regiment under camouflage netting during the build-up to the 1991 Gulf War. *(National Archives and Records Administration)*

This M109 was photographed recently with Ukrainian forces during their ongoing war with Russia. *(Creative Commons АрміяInform via Wikimedia Commons)*

in Vietnam. Cross-country travel was challenging, while its river crossing capability was minimal and it was not airmobile. Nevertheless, the M109 contributed significantly to the defence of forward operating bases in South Vietnam and supplied supporting firepower to infantry and armoured units engaged in critical battles in the north and central operational areas.

Since Vietnam, the M109 has undergone numerous improvements and upgrades, and its most recent version is expected to serve with the US armed forces into the 2030s. Other nations have operated the 'Paladin' in combat, including the Israeli Defence Force in the 1973 Yom Kippur War and the incursions into Lebanon in 1982 and 2006, the Iranian Army during the Iran-Iraq War of the late 1980s, the armies of numerous coalition nations during the 1991 Gulf War and US armed forces during Operation Iraqi Freedom in 2003.

The M109 remains in service today with many countries, although some have elected to replace the type with the German Panzerhaubitze 2000. ■

This M109A1 Paladin self-propelled howitzer is shown during 1982 exercises in Germany. *(US Government)*

M110
SELF-PROPELLED HOWITZER

The size of the 8in howitzer mounted with the M110 is readily apparent in this photo taken circa 1950. *(Dutch Ministry of Defence)*

A stalwart of the Vietnam era, the M110 self-propelled howitzer remains in service with several countries more than 60 years after its introduction. *(Creative Commons 100yen via Wikimedia Commons)*

The M110 self-propelled howitzer was developed for the US Army in the 1950s concurrently with the M107, which shared an identical chassis and gun mount. While the M107 carried a 175mm gun, the M110 served as the platform for the M115 203mm howitzer.

The Pacific Car & Foundry Company undertook production in 1962, and the M110 was accepted into service the following year with the US Army and US Marine Corps. FMC Corporation and Bowen-McLaughlin-York also produced the M110 during the later years of its run. Revisions resulted in the M110A1 in the mid-1970s, with a longer barrel for increased range, and the M110A2 with a double muzzle break for the howitzer. At one time, the M110 was the largest serviceable self-propelled howitzer in the US Army. It was deployed in Vietnam as a long-range infantry and armour support weapon capable of destroying enemy bunkers and exposed troop concentrations, while also being adept at counter-battery fire.

The M110 was powered by the 405hp, eight-cylinder Detroit Diesel 8V71T turbocharged engine, generating a top speed of 34mph with a 325-mile range. The vehicle weighed 31 tons and was more than 10ft high and 35ft wide. The crew of 13 included the commander, driver and three gunners aboard the M110, while the remainder accompanied any deployment aboard an M548 tracked cargo carrier, which also transported 8in ammunition. Affixed to the roof of the chassis, the gun mount provided little protection for the crew against small-arms fire or shell splinters with only a half-inch of armour forward. That arrangement was justified due to the distance of the M110 from the front lines, which diminished the possibility of direct contact with the enemy.

The M2A1E1 howitzer was fired using separately loaded propellant or 'bagged' charges. These were the M1 Green Bag or M3 White Bag. The Green Bag was used to engage targets up to about 11,000 yards, while the White Bag was typically utilised against targets beyond 9,700 yards to maximum range of more than 23,000 yards. Due to the overlap, specific instructions were often necessary concerning which bag to insert in the breech as the artillery unit's fire direction centre identified distance-to-target on a scale of one to seven. Therefore, intermediate range targets might require some degree of discernment as to the appropriate charge. A large spade was deployed to the rear of the M110 to offset the considerable recoil of the big howitzer.

In Vietnam, the heavy firepower of the M110 was often critical to the outcome of a battle. Such was the case during the siege of Khe Sanh in early 1968. Criticism centred on the weapon's lack of range, which was rectified with the introduction of the M110A1.

The longevity of the M110 with the US military stretched to the M110A2 deployment during the 1991 Gulf War, and it was thereafter retired followingh the introduction of the M270 Multiple Launch Rocket System (MLRS). It remains in service with some countries today. ◼

The breech of the 8in howitzer of the M110A2, last variant of the self-propelled artillery vehicle. *(Creative Commons 玄史生 via Wikimedia Commons)*

M42 DUSTER

As the Cold War progressed, many senior US Army officers concluded that the speed and manoeuvrability of jet aircraft had rendered the anti-aircraft gun obsolete. However, by the early 1960s, the American experience in Vietnam had caused a rethink. The early variant of the MIM-23 Hawk medium-range surface-to-air missile was not effective against targets at lower altitudes.

One temporary solution was to bring back the M42, a self-propelled anti-aircraft package that mounted a pair of M2A1 Bofors 40mm guns with a rate of fire of 240 rounds per minute (336 rounds were routinely aboard). The M42 was a direct descendant of the M19 multiple gun motor carriage that mounted the identical M2A1 dual 40mm guns atop the chassis of the M24 Chaffee light tank. In the midst of armed conflict in Korea from 1950-1953, the army decided to phase out the M24 in favour of the new M41 Walker Bulldog and all derivatives of the Chaffee that used that chassis went with it.

However, the 40mm anti-aircraft guns were still considered viable in defence against low-flying enemy jets, so a modified version of the existing 40mm gun mount was married to the chassis of the M41 to produce the M42 self-propelled anti-aircraft gun. General Motors produced the M42 from 1952 to 1959 at its Cleveland Tank Plant and approximately 3,700 were completed. The weapon system entered service in 1953. However, by 1963, the new wave of tactical thinking ended active deployment of the M42 in favour of the Hawk – until involvement in Vietnam flipped the script.

The M42 was powered by a 500hp, six-cylinder Continental or Lycoming engine that produced a top speed of 45mph and an operational range of 99 miles. It weighed just under 25 tons fully loaded and was operated by a crew of four to six, including a commander, driver and up to four men who serviced the weapon in combat from the open gun mount. Secondary armament consisted of a single light machine gun. When the deficiency with the early

The crew of an M42 'Duster' pulls security duty along Route 9 in Vietnam, 1968. *(Creative Commons From the Robert L. Drieslein Collection (COLL/5643) at the Archives Branch, Marine Corps History Division via Wikimedia Commons)*

Hawk was discovered, the M42 was given a new powerplant, designated the M42A1, and deployed in three battalions of the army's Air Defense Artillery detachment to Vietnam.

The first M42s reached Southeast Asia in the autumn of 1966 with the 1st Battalion, 44th Artillery, and though there were relatively few opportunities to shoot down enemy aircraft, the vehicle found a new vocation. The rapid-fire 40mm Bofors proved deadly in the ground support role, so the M42 crews found themselves involved with convoy escort, perimeter security and direct fire missions. Soon enough, the M42 was dubbed 'Duster' by American soldiers because its effective fire literally turned enemy troops into dust. The M42 served with distinction in Vietnam and memorably led the relief column that reached the forward base at Khe Sanh in early 1968, effectively ending the 77-day siege.

The three 'Duster' battalions were returned to the US in December 1971, with most of the remaining M42s handed to South Vietnamese forces. Others were detailed to National Guard units, the last being retired in 1988. ■

The M42 Duster mounted a pair of 40mm Bofors guns, which made it a deadly ground support weapon in Vietnam. *(Creative Commons avyakata via Wikimedia Commons)*

An M42 'Duster' at a US Army compound, Quang Tri City, Vietnam, in February 1968. *(Creative Commons Sciacchitano via Wikimedia Commons)*

M50 ONTOS

Looks can be deceiving and the consequences of underestimating an armoured fighting vehicle can be grave for the enemy. Such was the case with the M50 Ontos. Officially designated the Rifle, Multiple 106mm self-propelled M50, it was an unusual looking machine of war that was nonetheless adept at traversing the rice paddies, swamps and riverine shallows of Vietnam.

Translated from the Greek, its name literally means 'thing'. And when the time came for the Ontos to shine, it was indeed up to the task.

A product of the early days of the Cold War, the M50 Ontos was intended as a light, mobile anti-tank vehicle. Designed by machinery manufacturer Allis-Chalmers in 1952, the Ontos entered production in 1955 and fewer than 300 were built in a two-year run. The vehicle mounted a cast steel turret with two arms that each supported three of its six 105mm M40 recoilless rifles, which were officially designated as 106mm to prevent confusion with the earlier M27 recoilless rifle, which the M40 actually replaced.

Manned by a crew of three, the Ontos utilised the chassis of the earlier M56 Scorpion anti-tank vehicle and was fully tracked. Its six-cylinder 145hp General Motors petrol engine produced a top speed of 30mph and a range of 115 miles. At 19,000 pounds, the vehicle was light and even air transportable. Four of the recoilless rifles were equipped with BAT M8C .50-calibre single-shot spotting rifles that fired tracer rounds for target acquisition, and a .30-calibre Browning M1919 machine gun was placed atop the turret for close defence. After initial testing of the prototype in 1955, the US Army cancelled its contract, but the US Marine Corps remained involved and received the first operational Ontos on October 31, 1956.

During the 1965 build-up of US forces, the Marines sent two battalions of Ontos to Vietnam. Although the M50 was not destined to play its intended role since armoured clashes were

The M50 Ontos gave US Marines close infantry support during critical battles in Vietnam. *(US Army)*

relatively uncommon, it was discovered that the heavy firepower and manoeuvrability of the vehicle made it ideal for close infantry support. During the Tet Offensive of early 1968, the Ontos was invaluable in the fight for the provincial capital of Hue. One Marine officer described it as the most effective infantry support weapon available, blasting holes in walls and other obstructions and even collapsing buildings as the Marines cleared the old citadel section of the city.

Meanwhile, as the fight for Hue raged, the American combat base at Khe Sanh came

An American Marine sleeps atop an M50 Ontos during a lull in the fighting at Hue, 1968. *(US Marine Corps Archives via Wikimedia Commons)*

under attack. MH-53 transport helicopters airlifted 10 Ontos to the besieged position, and they turned in a stellar performance. North Vietnamese and Viet Cong troops came to fear the Ontos and sometimes took to their heels at the sight of it. The M50 was highly effective at reducing enemy bunkers and machine gun positions, while it also fired an anti-personnel round known as a 'beehive' that released 10,000 small steel flechettes that annihilated enemy troop concentrations.

By the time the fighting at Hue and Khe Sanh concluded, the Ontos was nearing the end of its service life in Vietnam due to operational fatigue and absence of spare parts. The last Ontos was withdrawn from action in the spring of 1969. The few that remained were assigned to an army light infantry brigade. ■

An M50 Ontos sits at a base in Vietnam in 1967. The Ontos provided close infantry support at Hue and Khe Sanh. *(US Marine Archives via Wikimedia Commons)*

M56 SCORPION

An M56 Scorpion on display at the Texas Military Forces Museum. *(Creative Commons Pi3.124)*

American military planners realised that airmobile combat capability would be enhanced with the addition of a light, self-propelled anti-tank weapon that could provide support against enemy armour. Development of such a platform began in the late 1940s and, by 1955, the prototype T101 had been completed.

The T101 entered production in 1957 as the M56 Scorpion self-propelled gun, with the Cadillac Motor Car Division of General Motors completing about 325 during a run that lasted two years. The M56 was developed with the understanding that at least one of the three basic components of an effective armoured fighting vehicle – speed, firepower and armour protection – would necessarily be compromised in the finished design. Firepower would remain a key component, and that requirement was filled adequately with the 90mm M54 high velocity gun and 29 rounds of ammunition. No secondary armament was installed.

Speed was to be provided by the Continental AOI-403-5 petrol engine that generated 200hp, a top speed of 28mph and an operational range of 140 miles. Further, the manoeuvrability of the Scorpion was enhanced by its fully tracked chassis in combination with four road tyres. The dual running system reduced the overall weight of the vehicle to 16,000lb and decreased its ground pressure. Therefore, the M56 was quite agile in sand, mud, snow and marshland – even the rice paddies of Vietnam.

The necessary sacrifice of armour is readily apparent in the minimal protection provided the crew of four, which including a commander, gunner, driver and loader. The vehicle was essentially unarmoured with the exception of the blast shield, which was only 5mm thick. As the crew compartment was open, there was no secondary protection, making the M56 quite vulnerable to enemy return fire. Its best defence after discharging the 90mm gun was to displace

to one of several predetermined locations to reload and re-enter a combat situation.

The discharge of the 90mm weapon, with its semi-automatic action that opened the breech and ejected the spent shell, was in itself somewhat problematic. Its substantial recoil shook the entire vehicle rather violently, causing the crew to become briefly disoriented and even lifting the entire chassis off the ground. A pair of recuperators was installed to reduce the recoil, but had little effect.

A company of 16 M56s was deployed to South Vietnam with the US Army's 173rd Airborne Brigade, which was the only airborne unit to field the weapon during the conflict. Since tank vs tank encounters were rare in Southeast Asia, the Scorpion became primarily a close infantry support weapon. The subsequent availability of the M551 Sheridan rendered the M56 functionally obsolete and it was withdrawn from frontline service in the early 1970s. ■

An M56 Scorpion is shown in Vietnam operating with M113 armoured personnel carriers. *(Cunneen, William James Australian Government via Wikimedia Commons)*

The 90mm gun of the M56 Scorpion is prominent in this image from the War Memorial of Korea. *(Creative Commons User:Piotrus via Wikimedia Commons)*

M132 FLAMETHROWER

Thai soldiers operate an M132 flamethrower against Viet Cong positions in November 1967. *(National Archives and Records Administration)*

M132 armoured flamethrower tank on display at the War Remnants Museum in Ho Chi Minh City, Vietnam. *(Creative Commons Panda 51 via Wikimedia Commons)*

Following the combat experience of the US Army and Marine Corps with the flamethrower variant of the M4 Sherman medium tank during World War Two, both branches of the armed forces sought to continue the availability of such mobile firepower during the years of the Cold War and Vietnam. The Army Chemical Corps' Chemical Research and Development Laboratories began work on such a project in June 1954.

The M132, nicknamed 'Zippo' after the popular cigarette lighter of the period, was based on the chassis of the M113 Armored Personnel Carrier. Its two-man crew included a driver, who was posted forward and to the left in the hull, and a gunner, whose position was in a small cupola modified from the M1 cupola of the M48 and M60 tanks. The cupola retained a 7.62mm coaxial machine gun to the right with the M8 flame projector to the left. The M8 was fed by the M10 combination fuel and pressure unit located inside the converted personnel space of the standard M113.

An earlier programme to equip the preceding M59 Armored Personnel Carrier with a flamethrower was discarded, but three prototypes with the M113 were built. Testing was completed at Fort Benning, Georgia, and Fort Greeley, Alaska, in 1961. Food Machinery Corporation built 351 self-propelled flamethrower vehicles designated M132 with a petrol engine and the later M132A1 with a diesel powerplant. By late 1964, the Army Concept Team in Vietnam recommended the attachment of four M132s and a pair of M113s to each armoured cavalry regiment in country.

Like the M113, the armour protection of the M132 was quite thin, so it was operated in co-operation with screening infantry. To achieve the best results, suppressing machine-gun fire would be levelled on a target to allow the vehicle to advance within range of its flame weapon, roughly 186 yards. A wet burst of fuel was followed moments later by a streak of flame. In one incident, witnesses described the destruction of a Viet Cong 57mm recoilless rifle position with a three-second burst of flame during combat at Ap Tau O in June 1966.

Concurrently with the M132, the Marine Corps pursued another self-propelled flamethrower, which became its standard weapon of the type in Vietnam. Also nicknamed 'Zippo', the M67 flamethrower tank was a modification of the M48 by mounting an M7-6 flamethrower gun rather than the 90mm cannon. The US government's Detroit Arsenal, under operational direction of the Chrysler Corporation, produced 109 M67s during the 1950s, while 76 were converted from the M48A3 at the Anniston and Red River Army Depots in 1963-1964.

After the Vietnam conflict, the US armed forces de-emphasised the role of self-propelled flamethrower vehicles, citing the changing face of modern combat. Both the M132 and M67 remained in reserve until the 1970s. ∎

An M132 flamethrower spews a stream of fire while clearing a landing zone with troopers of the 1st Cavalry Division (Airmobile). *(US Army)*

Serving in the ground support role, M163 Vulcans give soldiers a ride as they embark on a search and destroy mission in Vietnam. *(US Army)*

M163 VULCAN AIR DEFENSE SYSTEM

The versatility of the M113 Armored Personnel Carrier led to numerous applications, including air defence. In the early 1960s, the US Army explored the pairing of a new generation of surface-to-air missiles along with a conventional gun platform. It was reasoned that together these systems might constitute a complementary defence against aircraft from low to medium altitude, particularly enemy attack helicopters armed with anti-tank weapons.

The chassis of the M113 was chosen for both the new MIM-72A/M48 Chaparral missile system and the M163 Vulcan Air Defense System (VADS), which was intended to replace the M46 'Duster'. The Chaparral system carried a surface-to-air adaptation of the heat-seeking air-to-air AIM-9 Sidewinder missile, while the M163 mounted the General Dynamics M168 20mm rotary cannon, commonly referred to as a 'Gatling Gun' and already in use aboard some US-manufactured combat aircraft.

The chassis and internal components of the M113 were largely unchanged in the M163, while the Chapparal was modified to accommodate the missile launcher with a forward cab and designated the M730 vehicle (adapted by Ford Motor Company, the M730 was officially a variant of the M113A1). A crew of four, including a commander, gunner, loader and driver, operated the M163, while two men were sufficient for the Chaparral. In May 1969, the first Chaparral battalion arrived in Vietnam and at least 1,100 of the systems were completed in the 1960s.

Design work on the Vulcan was undertaken by General Electric in 1964, and production of the standard M163 and improved models

This M163 Vulcan was damaged by the explosion of a Viet Cong mortar round in the Vietnamese jungle. *(US Army)*

An American soldier inspects the barrels of the 20mm rotary cannon mounted on an M163 Vulcan anti-aircraft gun system in Vietnam, January 1969. *(US Army)*

continued at various intervals from 1965 to 1982. The original Vulcan was powered by the 212hp General Motors 6V53 diesel engine with a top speed of 40mph and a range of 298 miles. The M163 weighed 13.8 tons fully loaded.

The M168 20mm cannon was capable of an astounding rate of fire, up to 3,000 rounds per minute, as well as a minimum rate of 1,000 rounds per minute in bursts of 10, 30, 60 or 100 rounds; 2,100 rounds were usually carried aboard. The M168's effective range was just over three miles. It was capable of firing a variety of shells, including high explosive/incendiary and armour piercing discarding sabot (APDS).

The M163 was intended to carry onboard radar, but when the first examples were delivered to Vietnam in 1969, only dummy equipment had been installed. In the temporary absence of radar, targets were acquired by sight, thus the M163 was engaged in ground support. Its tracked chassis gave the Vulcan enhanced manoeuvrability compared to wheeled vehicles, and its cross-country capability was a welcome addition during infantry operations.

Serviceable radar was introduced as it became available and upgrades to the original M163 occurred periodically through the decades. Among the most significant of these was the PIVADS (Product Improved VADS) project of 1984, which introduced improved targeting and operational characteristics.

Replacement weapons developed in recent years include the M1097 Avenger and the M6 Linebacker. The last Vulcan in service with the US Army was retired in 1994. ◼

M3 SCOUT CAR

M3 Scout Car of the Guards Armoured Division in 1942. *(Collections of the Imperial War Museums)*

I n the mid-1930s, the White Motor Company of Cleveland, Ohio, offered one of the first vehicles to provide mechanisation on a wide scale for the US military. Testing of the M1 Scout Car took place in 1934. The M2 followed in 1935 and, from there, a redesigned vehicle emerged two years later.

Essentially a light armoured truck, the basic M3 design was completed by 1937. It featured a four-wheel-drive chassis from White along with a superstructure with up to a half-inch of armour protection manufactured by another Ohio-based enterprise, the Diebold Safe and Lock Company.

The simple construction of the M3 facilitated its acceptance by the US Army and more than 22,000 were built between 1939 and 1944. Armour protection was considered adequate against infantry small-arms fire, while reliance on speed compensated for any perceived deficiency. That speed was delivered by the 110hp, six-cylinder Hercules JDX gasoline engine, producing a top road speed of 55mph and a range of 250 miles. A wheelbase of nearly 10ft provided stability on difficult roadways and terrain, and the engine and other vital components were protected with steel plating. The fully loaded vehicle weighed nearly six tons.

A crew of three, comprising a commander, driver and gunner, operated the M3, while the rear section was built with six bucket seats. Both cab and passenger compartment were open-topped and could be covered with canvas tarpaulins. The armament of the M3 consisted of the Browning .50-calibre M2 heavy machine gun mounted above the centre of the vehicle and a skate rail allowed the weapon to be moved around the perimeter of the crew area. It was common to also install a .30-calibre Browning M1919 machine gun for additional firepower.

Revisions to the original design and equipment of the M3 occurred during testing and deployment, with the M3A1 becoming the main production variant by 1940. Important modifications for the M3A1 used by the US and other Allied forces during World War Two included a lengthened hull, an unditching roller mounted on the front bumper, the standard addition of two M1919 machine guns for a total of three onboard weapons, the introduction of the skate rail for the M2 machine gun and improved radio communications equipment. The overwhelming number of M3s produced were of the M3A1 variant.

The M3A1 was used widely during World War Two in the supply, transport, ambulance and reconnaissance roles. However, by1943, the type was largely supplanted by the M8 armoured car and M20 utility car. After the war ended, surplus M3A1s were distributed to many countries. France utilised the vehicle during its fight against the communist Viet Minh and, after the European withdrawal, South Vietnamese forces employed the M3A1 as well. The Dominican Republic maintained the last of type in service into the 1990s. ■

US General George S Patton Jr peers from his open-topped M3A1 during World War Two. *(US Army)*

M3A1 Scout Car modified to carry a 37mm gun. The M3A1 was adapted to at least four additional configurations. *(US Army)*

M3 HALFTRACK

M3 halftrack anti-aircraft variant in a bleak landscape during the Korean War. *(US Army)*

The M3 Scout Car was the progenitor of the famed M3 Halftrack that became an icon among armoured vehicles of the Allied forces during World War Two and survived the war in such large numbers that it remained in use for years afterward. The M3 Halftrack was produced from 1941 through 1945, including well over a dozen variants as more than 54,000 were built.

The French military deployed the M3 during its abortive Indochina foray from 1946 to 1954, while as many as 20 countries brought it into service during and after World War Two.

The development of an American-made halftrack, so called due to its forward wheeled chassis and tracked chassis to the rear, began with US Army Ordnance Directive OCM 1488 specifying the conversion of the existing M3 Scout Car into a halftrack as a reconnaissance vehicle and prime mover. White Motor Company, which had developed the original scout car, collaborated with Rock Island Arsenal to develop the T7 prototype, but tests conducted in 1938 were disappointing. However, further experimentation led to the prototype T14, which served as the template for the M2 Halftrack, immediate predecessor of the M3.

Many components were common to the M3 Scout Car and the M2 and M3 Halftracks, and the family resemblance is obvious. More than 11,000 examples of the M2 were built during World War Two by the White Motor and Autocar, with some surplus M2s also deployed by the French in Vietnam. The M2 served as a platform for further evolution of the halftrack. While it functioned in its original roles, the vehicle provided only enough space for the addition of a gun crew when it served as a prime mover.

By 1940, the larger M3 had been developed to accommodate a complement of 13 fully loaded combat troops. White and Autocar were joined in production of the M3 by the Diamond Motor Car Company. An export version was built by International Harvester and supplied to Allied countries through Lend-Lease.

The early M3 was powered by the 148hp, six-cylinder White 160 Ax petrol engine with a top speed of 45mph and a range of 200 miles. Other more powerful engines were introduced over time. Armament was similar to the M2, with a .50-calibre Browning M2 heavy machine gun in a pintle mount that was later changed to

M3 Halftrack on display at a museum in Ursel, Belgium. *(Creative Commons Paul Hermans via Wikimedia Commons)*

A column of M3 Halftracks during manoeuvres at Fort Knox, Kentucky. *(US Army)*

a ring mount, along with two pintle-mounted .30-calibre Browning Model 1919 machine guns. Just over 20ft long, the M3 weighed eight tons.

The M3 was open overhead, offering no protection against shrapnel and shell fragments, but more armour plating was applied in the M3A1 by 1941, increasing the vehicle's weight to nearly 8½ tons. Nevertheless, subsequent combat experience suggested its thin armour protection was vulnerable to basic German MG34 and MG42 machine-gun rounds, leading to the M3 and its variants being given the nickname 'Purple Heart Boxes'.

Early mechanical issues were addressed soon after deployment during World War Two and the M3 then earned a reputation as rugged and reliable in the field. ∎

M8 GREYHOUND

The role of the M8 Greyhound evolved through its long career, spanning the World War Two era into the 1980s.

In the late 1930s, the US Army's best anti-tank vehicle was the M6 Gun Motor Carriage, essentially a Dodge WC series light truck with an M3 37mm anti-tank gun, the first American weapon of its kind, mounted in its bed. The inherent deficiencies of the M6 prompted the US Army Ordnance Department to issue specifications for a replacement in the summer of 1941, even though production of the M6 continued for the duration of World War Two.

Studebaker, Chrysler and Ford all submitted prototypes in response to the Ordnance Department directive, with the Ford T22E1 design being adopted. The new M8 was later dubbed 'Greyhound' by its British users.

A leap forward from the primitive M6, the M8 was a wheeled 6X6 vehicle with a welded hull and turret which mounted the 37mm anti-tank main gun. Secondary armament consisted of a .50-calibre Browning M2 machine gun and a single .30-calibre Browning M1919 machine gun. The crew consisted of the commander and gunner in the turret and the driver and radio operator forward in the hull, seated left and right respectively.

Armour protection was minimal at just one inch, a deterrent to engaging the M8 in direct infantry support missions, and crews tried to compensate for the vulnerability to small-arms fire with sandbags. The vehicle was particularly susceptible to land mines and sandbags were routinely packed into the floor for some absorption of a potentially catastrophic blast. The Greyhound was powered by the 110hp, six-cylinder Hercules JXD engine delivering a top road speed of 30mph and range of up to 400 miles with stored petrol. Although the vehicle was all-wheel-drive, its performance off-road, particularly in thick or muddy terrain, was deemed suboptimal. From March 1943 through June 1945, Ford Motor Company built more than 8,500 Greyhounds.

The M8 entered service with the US Army during the World War Two Sicily campaign

An M8 Greyhound participating in World War Two commemorative activities. *(Creative Commons Alf van Beem via Wikimedia Commons)*

This M8 Greyhound scout car was retired from service with the French Army. *(Creative Commons Domenjod via Wikimedia Commons)*

US soldiers manning an M8 scout car greet medical personnel during World War Two. Note the chains on the M8's tyres. *(US Army)*

in 1943, and given that its 37mm gun was incapable of penetrating the thick armour of improved German tanks such as the PzKpfw. V Panther and PzKpfw. VI Tiger, its role became restricted to reconnaissance rather than that of tank destroyer. Many M8s were detailed to the Pacific, where they were a match for anything the Japanese fielded in armoured vehicles.

France became the largest post-war operator of the M8 and its primary variant, the M20 utility car (turretless and built for command and control). The French Army took possession of many armoured cars that were shipped directly from the US to Southeast Asia and used them primarily for reconnaissance. When the French departed in the mid-1950s, remaining M8s were handed to the South Vietnamese armed forces. These remained in service in Vietnam through the mid-1960s until the replacement M706 or Cadillac Gage Commando began arriving in country.

At least 48 countries operated the M8 during the Cold War as numerous modifications and modernisation programmes kept the vehicle relevant and cheaper than the production or purchase of tanks. ∎

M59 ARMORED PERSONNEL CARRIER

M59 Armored Personnel Carrier on display at Aberdeen Proving Ground, Maryland. *(Creative Commons Mark Pellegrini via Wikimedia Commons)*

Even as the M75 Armored Personnel Carrier was at war in Korea, carrying US and United Nations troops into action, work on its replacement was proceeding apace. As early as 1951, the Food Machinery and Chemical Corporation (FMC), manufacturer of the M75, was at work on its successor.

The subsequent prototype T59 was accepted by the US Army for production in June 1953 and designated officially as the M59 Armored Personnel Carrier (APC). It offered distinct advantages over the M75 as it was cheaper to produce, its profile was lower at just over nine feet presenting a smaller target to enemy forces and it did not require the installation of a fording kit for amphibious operations in shallow water.

The M75's career was shortlived. Although it was proven to be reliable in the field and utilised the chassis of the M41 Walker Bulldog light tank, only 1,729 were completed between December 1952 and February 1954. When the M59 became available, the surplus M75s were given to the Belgian Army, serving into the 1980s.

Approximately 6,300 M59s had been built when its production run ended in 1960. The vehicle entered service in the spring of 1954 and was utilised widely during the early years of the Vietnam war, but was supplanted by the follow-on M113, which arrived in country beginning in the spring of 1962. Both the M75 and M59 heavily influenced the better-known M113, as evidenced by the physical resemblance.

The design of the M59 was box-like with some slope to the glacis, less armour protection than the M75 at nearly an inch forward, 5/8ths of an inch on the flanks, rear and underside and 3/8ths of an inch on the roof, which made the vehicle lighter at just over 21 tons. Armament included a single .50-calibre Browning M2 machine gun positioned at the commander's cupola, while an automatic weapon or carbine was often stored for close action. The interior of the M59 was a single space, while the roof was configured in three sections. The front section included the driver's hatch to the left and commander's cupola on the right.

The cargo space included benches on either side to accommodate 10 fully loaded combat troops. This seating could be folded to allow space for additional cargo, an artillery piece or a small vehicle. One notable variant was the M84 mortar carrier, which was modified to mount the 4.2-inch mortar in the floor of the cargo area.

The powerplant of the M59 consisted of twin 146hp, six-cylinder GMC petrol engines that produced a top road speed of 32mph, considerably slower than the M75 (43mph), and a range of 120 miles. The performance of

An M84 variant of the M59 moves into firing position with Troop B, 3rd Squadron, 4th Cavalry Regiment, 25th Infantry Division, during Operation Cedar Falls, Vietnam 1967. *(US Army)*

the twin engines suffered in the humid climate of Vietnam, creating maintenance issues.

Although its tenure in frontline service was relatively short, the M59 remained active in the US Army reserve components until the 1980s. It was exported to numerous countries during the 1960s and 1970s. ∎

M59s pass in review during President John F Kennedy's inauguration, January 20, 1961. *(United States Government)*

M113 ARMORED PERSONNEL CARRIER

Mechanised warfare demands the ability to transport combat soldiers swiftly and with a modicum of protection into the teeth of the fight. The so-called 'battle taxi' concept was in its infancy in World War Two, but matured somewhat in the US Army during the early 1950s with the M75 and M59 Armored Personnel Carriers, then came to fruition in the Vietnam era with the M113.

The M113 Armored Personnel Carrier (APC) is perhaps the best-known of any armoured vehicle of the Vietnam conflict. Film footage and photos of it in action in the jungles or traversing rice paddies abound. The longevity of the M113 and its abundant variations is remarkable, and the vehicle was first accepted into service with the US Army in 1960. Production continued through many upgrades and variants until 2007, with approximately 80,000 built during that time.

The M113 made its combat debut with the South Vietnamese armed forces in the spring of 1962. During fighting around Ap Bac in January 1963, several vehicles were lost when gunners manning the exposed .50-calibre Browning machine guns took heavy casualties.

An M113 in the ACAV role advancing through heavy bush while leading a combined arms attack in Vietnam. *(US Army)*

As a result, the Army of the Republic of Vietnam (ARVN) set about modifying the original M113 with shields for the machine-gunners, more weapons and additional armour protection. The ARVN modifications transformed the role of the M113 from battle taxi to that of a light tank. Prevailing US Army doctrine specified that the two-man crew, a commander and driver, would discharge their human cargo of 11 combat soldiers and retire. However, the ARVN M113s hit the North Vietnamese and Viet Cong with everything they had, working with the infantry and other armoured vehicles. Depending on the source consulted, either the ARVN soldiers who rode into firefights with the M113 or the Viet Cong guerrillas who opposed them began calling the vehicle the 'Green Dragon'.

The M113 had come about during the 1950s as the Army sought improvements to the M75 and M59, both of which had favourable points but substantial performance issues. The new requirement was for an APC that was airmobile, armoured, amphibious and multi-purpose. Previously engaged in APC

M113 ACAVs of the 3rd Battalion, 11th Cavalry Regiment, attack in a herringbone formation during Operation Cedar Falls in Vietnam. *(US Army)*

Troopers of the 173rd Airborne Brigade fire 4.2-in mortar rounds at the Viet Cong during Operation Waco, Vietnam. *(Creative Commons WWW3ii via Wikimedia Commons)*

US Army troops exit an M113 during exercises in 1985. *(US Department of Defense)*

development, the Food Machinery and Chemical Corporation stepped up with two prototypes, one heavier in steel construction and the other made of 5083 aircraft-grade aluminium alloy developed in partnership with the Kaiser Aluminum and Chemical Company in the late 1950s. The T113 aluminium prototype was lighter and received the approval of the military for production. An improved prototype designated T113E1 was officially adopted as the M113.

The early powerplant consisted of a 260hp, eight-cylinder Chrysler 75M petrol engine delivering a top speed of more than 40mph and a range of 200 miles. However, by 1964, tendencies of the petrol engine to catch fire meant it was replaced by a General Motors 215hp diesel unit. The diesel-powered vehicle was designated the M113A1.

The M113 presented a significant profile, with a height of more than eight feet, width of nearly nine feet and length just short of 16 feet. Its original aluminium armour varied from just over one inch to 1.7in in thickness, meaning it weighed slightly more than 12 tons. The vehicle included roof hatches for

loading cargo, and a large ramp was used for troop ingress and egress from the rear.

Initially, US advisors were taken aback by the new ARVN application of the M113s in combat, but they embraced the concept that came to be known as the Armored Cavalry Assault Vehicle (ACAV). More M113s were modified with additional armour protection in the form of steel plating bolted to the belly and flanks, while sandbags were placed on the decks to improve resistance to land mines and stand-off mesh armour was installed to diminish the impact of rocket-propelled grenades.

Armament upgrades included a pair of light .30-calibre machine guns, recoilless rifles, flamethrowers and even a 20mm rapid-fire cannon that spawned the M163 Vulcan variant.

As the American commitment to ground forces in Vietnam increased substantially by 1965, many M113s and M113A1s joined the troops in country and undertook the ACAV role. The unit history of the 25th Infantry Division recounts the perspective of Lieutenant Colonel Louis J North, commander of the 4th Battalion, 23rd Infantry Regiment, on the expected performance of the M113 ACAV. He commented in January 1967 that the armoured fighting vehicle would "enhance the mobility and shock action of the battalion... It will simplify the problems of going into heavily booby-trapped areas and give us the ability to close in on the enemy and with greater firepower."

Meanwhile, the M113 continued to perform its intended task, delivering combat troops to the battlefield, while also serving as an improvised ambulance for the evacuation of wounded and as a cargo transport. However, in action, the vehicle took losses. According to reports, between November 1967 and March 1970, a total of 1,342 M113s were destroyed due to enemy action, and an estimated 73% of all vehicle losses during the period were attributed to communist land mines buried in fields and along roadways.

The M113 and its many variants left an indelible mark on the American experience in Vietnam, as well as that of its allies. The type continued through numerous performance upgrades and was deployed with US mechanised infantry units through the 1980s as its replacements, the M2 and M3 Bradley infantry and cavalry fighting vehicles, became available. The US armed forces have maintained the M113 in various support roles into the 21st Century and the so-called War on Terror. Meanwhile, more than 50 countries have counted the M113 in their armoured vehicle inventories. ■

The seating area for combat troops in transport aboard an M113. *(Yellowute public domain via Wikipedia)*

Crewmen operate the three machine guns aboard an M113 ACAV as they prepare to cross a stream in Vietnam, 1966. *(US Army)*

M577 COMMAND POST CARRIER

The distinguishing raised roof section of the M577 Command Post Carrier. *(Creative Commons Italian Army via Wikimedia Commons)*

During the early years of the Cold War, senior US military officers realised that modern combined arms ground operations required enhanced command and control. By definition, a successful ground operation would lead to the expansion of the battlefield's size and the scope and tactical missions of the units involved. Further, it was noted that command and control could not necessarily remain in a stationary position as operations progressed.

By the early 1960s, the US Army had taken steps to ensure mobile command and control capability between infantry, armour and artillery, particularly at the battalion level. The solution lay in the already familiar M113 Armored Personnel Carrier (APC), which provided the space necessary for personnel to operate radio communications, refer to maps, co-ordinate deployments and, if necessary, serve as a fire direction centre. This resulted in one of the most critical modifications to the base M113.

By February 1962, four identical XM577 prototype command and control vehicles converted from the M113 were produced at the Detroit Arsenal. In March of that year, these were distributed to the Aberdeen Proving Ground, Maryland, and other locations under the auspices of the artillery, armour and infantry boards for evaluation. Good results led to the approval of an initial production run of 270 vehicles. These were placed in service with the US Army by March 1963 and, within weeks, the first examples were on their way to Vietnam.

Another order for 674 vehicles was placed after the XM577 became officially recognised as the Carrier, Command Post, Light Tracked M577. Through numerous upgrades and civilian contract producers through the decades, more than 7,300 examples have been manufactured, and the M577 remains in service today.

Although the M577 clearly resembled its progenitor, the new vehicle differed from the M113 in several aspects. The upper section of the hull and the sides were extended by more than two feet above the standard, allowing the passenger compartment headroom to rise to nearly 6ft, 3in. An auxiliary power unit was mounted on the roof and the commander's cupola was removed in favour of a hatch. The higher roof space allowed up to three personnel to work inside while standing upright.

The M577 shared many of the same construction elements as the M113, which had been the first US armoured vehicle to enter service with an all-welded aluminium hull. The drivetrain, powerplant and chassis were identical and, in the simplest terms, the M577 was an M113 with a raised rear roof, the addition of radio and electronic communications equipment, folding tables, dome lighting, heating and cooling temperature controls, a rolled tent and framework mounted externally for deployment when the vehicle was stationary for any lengthy period.

One notable further modification of the M577 was the M1068 Standard Integrated Command Post System (SICPS) that followed the 1991 Gulf War and brought numerous enhancements in communications and other equipment. ■

An M577 is shown in the field with its headquarters tent deployed to the rear. *(US Army)*

A soldier uses communications equipment from the interior of an M577. *(US Government)*

M114
RECONNAISSANCE VEHICLE

Proposed as a light, manoeuvrable reconnaissance vehicle that was airmobile, amphibious and fast while also providing some degree of command and control in combat, the M114 rapidly proved a failure in the field. Although its close relative, the M113 Armored Personnel Carrier, served with distinction in Vietnam and gained lasting fame, it was not to be for the M114.

Acknowledging the utility and performance of the M113, the US Army engaged engineers of the General Motors' Cadillac Division to produce 1,214 T114 command and reconnaissance carriers. The two contracts totalled $14.9 million and production was undertaken with high expectations.

The vehicle was accepted into service in 1962 and designated the M114. Smaller than the M113, it weighed 7½ tons, stood nearly eight feet high and was just over 7½ feet wide. The hull presented a lower profile than the M113 and was also constructed from aluminium alloy. The crew of three included a commander seated in the hull to the right beneath a large cupola, the driver in the hull forward and to the left and an observer/gunner behind and to the left. The M114 was armed with a single .50-calibre Browning M2 machine gun above the commander's position, but he would be exposed to enemy fire above the open hatch when operating it. A 7.62mm M60 light machine gun was located on a pedestal within reach of the observer/gunner.

The M114 was driven by a 160hp Chevrolet V8 engine that produced a maximum speed of 36mph and a range of 275 miles. Like the M113, the M114's aluminium was somewhat effective against small arms and shell fragments at a maximum thickness of 1¾ inches, but the vehicle was terribly susceptible to land mines.

The M114 reached Vietnam in 1964 and was distributed to US and South Vietnamese armoured cavalry reconnaissance squadrons. From the beginning, mechanical issues were encountered, while the engine was deemed underpowered to tackle the difficult terrain of jungles, swamps, mountains and sandy coastal areas. It shortcomings readily apparent, the M114 was withdrawn from frontline units in South Vietnam and replaced as soon as possible with the M551 Sheridan reconnaissance tank or further deployment of the M113 Armored Cavalry Assault Vehicle. Production was suspended and the programme was cancelled with a year.

By November 1964, the M114 had been relegated to reserve roles in Vietnam, although it remained the primary vehicle of its type with NATO forces in Europe and US troops in South Korea for several years. In the early 1970s, General Creighton Abrams, commander of US forces in South Vietnam, called for the withdrawal of the M114, branding it a total failure. By 1979, the vehicle was retired from service with the US Army. ◾

A retired M114 in the livery of the US 11th Armored Cavalry Regiment. *(Creative Commons Jeff Kubina via Wikimedia Commons)*

The failed M114 bears a significant resemblance to the highly successful M113 Armored Personnel Carrier. *(Creative Commons Mike Peel via Wikimedia Commons)*

The M114 reconnaissance vehicle proved a dismal failure in Vietnam and was withdrawn. *(US Army)*

Lynx scout car on parade while in service with the Dutch Army in Indonesia, 1947. *(Dutch National Archives)*

LYNX SCOUT CAR

Produced from 1943 to 1945, the Lynx Scout Car was one of many vehicles of World War Two vintage that found their way to the war in Southeast Asia. The origin of the Lynx dates to 1938, when the British War Office issued specifications for a scouting and reconnaissance vehicle. Morris, BSA Cycles and Alvis responded, with the BSA prototype chosen for production and the first order placed for 172 vehicles in the spring of 1939. Actual production was detailed to Daimler, a subsidiary of BSA, and the nickname of the Alvis entrant, 'Dingo', was appropriated for the new type.

The original 4X4 Dingo, officially called the Car, Scout, Mark I, was powered by a 2.5-litre, 55hp, straight six-cylinder Daimler petrol engine capable of a top speed of 55mph. Its armour was nearly 1¼in thick forward and reduced to less than ½in on the flanks. The vehicle was agile, fast and demonstrated solid handling and a tight turning radius. A .303-calibre Bren light machine gun or an alternative Boys 13.9mm anti-tank rifle could be mounted atop the Dingo, and the crew of two included a driver and commander/gunner.

Even as the Dingo was at the prototype stage, BSA engineers realised the potential of the design and embarked on a programme to produce a somewhat larger 'light tank (wheeled)' that came to be known simply as the Daimler Armoured Car. By the time Dingo production ceased in 1945, a total of 6,626 had been built. The three-year run for the Daimler Armoured Car ended with 2,694 completed. The two types were deployed to France with the 4th Royal Northumberland Fusiliers in the spring of 1940 and were utilised throughout World War Two.

The demand for the two vehicles was high and when Daimler reached its productivity limit in 1943, Ford Canada in Windsor, Ontario, took to manufacturing another derivative labelled the Scout Car, Ford Mk. 1, which became popularly known as the Lynx. Through the end of World War Two, 3,255 of this variant were completed. The Ford version was a foot taller than the Dingo to accommodate the larger Ford transmission needed for its more powerful V8 engine.

The Dingo family of vehicles was popular and remained in service well beyond World War Two, while the US Army purchased 40 of the Lynx variant for use in Vietnam in scouting and reconnaissance roles. It proved rugged and adept in negotiating difficult terrain.

One Lynx underwent some experimentation with the installation of a turret for heavier weapons and a potential role in convoy protection. South Vietnamese troops also utilised the Lynx. The Dingo family remained in service into the 1970s with the forces of several countries and it is a popular collectible vehicle today. ■

An abandoned Dingo on the beach at Dieppe, France, after the failed 1942 raid on the coastal city during World War Two. *(Creative Commons Bundesarchiv Bild via Wikimedia Commons)*

Ford Canada-built Lynx scout car in Yad La-Shiryon Museum in Israel. *(Creative Commons Bukvoed assumed via Wikimedia Commons)*

C15TA ARMOURED TRUCK

provided some protection against shell fragments and small-arms fire. Bins extended outward from the rear and could be used to secure gear for travelling soldiers while also serving as fenders.

The C15TA stood eight feet high, was 7ft, 7in wide and weighed 4½ tons. The powerplant was the 100hp, six-cylinder GMC 270 petrol engine, generating a top speed of 40mph. It was crewed by a driver and co-driver, while the passenger space officially accommodated eight combat troops. Three hoops or arches spanned the personnel space to support a canvas tarpaulin that extended the entire length and could be securely tied. Entry and exit was through an armoured door at the rear.

A few C15TA trucks were available during the early phase of the Italian campaign in 1943, but sufficient numbers were built in time for the fighting in France and beyond during the last months of World War Two in Europe. The truck received praise from operators and combat soldiers alike, demonstrating good characteristics in the field. At times, it was paired with the Otter in complementary roles as a 'battle taxi' and fire support vehicle. The CT15A was also robust enough to serve as an artillery tractor and stood duty in the ambulance role.

The C15TA served widely in Southeast Asia until the end of the war in 1975, while numerous nations operated the vehicle throughout the 1960s. ■

This well preserved C15TA armoured truck is on display with the markings of the US Army. *(Creative Commons Joost J. Bakker from Ijmuiden via Wikimedia Commons)*

The interior of the C15TA was a rather tight space, although the seats were sometimes removed to give more room. *(Creative Commons AlfvanBeem via Wikimedia Commons)*

W hen British forces departed Southeast Asia at the end of World War Two, they left behind many of their Canadian-built C15TA armoured trucks. In turn, these rugged vehicles were put to use by the French in Indochina and later by the armies of both North and South Vietnam.

During the Canadian build-up for D-Day, the army sought an adequate armoured transport vehicle that could carry troops, ammunition and other cargo. The expectation that the CAPLAD three-ton armoured lorry would fulfil the requirements was dashed when it failed to meet minimum standards and its production was cancelled. In part, the Canadians depended on the British White M3 Scout Car, but production of that type was waning. So Canada turned to another option based on the Canadian Military Pattern (CMP) Chevrolet C15 Truck chassis and incorporating an armoured hull supplied by the Hamilton Bridge Company. General Motors Canada produced 3,961 examples of the C15TA at its assembly plant in Oshawa, Ontario, from 1943 to 1945.

The wheeled 4X4 C15TA, officially the 'Truck 15cwt, Armoured', was easily recognisable by its blunt nose, cab-over-engine configuration and relatively high ground clearance. The armour design was based on that of the Canadian GM Otter Light Reconnaissance Car, which was already in service and shared the common CMP truck chassis. The engineers considered the role of the vehicle as being a comparatively fast troop transport and built the C15TA with sloped armour ranging from ¼in to just over ½in thickness, which

Soldiers of Canada's Royal Hamilton Light Infantry are loaded aboard C15TA armoured trucks during the battle of the Scheldt Estuary in autumn 1944. *(Canadian Public Domain)*

LVTP5 AMPHIBIOUS ARMORED PERSONNEL CARRIER

LVTP5 on display in the military park near the battleship USS *Alabama* in the city of Mobile. *(Creative Commons Vitaly Barsov via Wikimedia Commons)*

Tracing its heritage back to the tracked landing vehicles that gained fame during World War Two in the Pacific, the LVTP5 (Landing Vehicle, Tracked, Personnel 5) Armored Personnel Carrier (APC) was a second-generation amphibious vehicle that incorporated lessons learned from its predecessors in action on the islands of Tarawa, the Marianas, Iwo Jima and Okinawa.

Colloquially called the 'Amtrac', these landing craft were first conceived to negotiate the coral reefs and other offshore hazards that impeded offensive landings against Japanese-held territory in the Pacific. The early Amtracs rapidly proved their worth as they were developed and refined during the conflict and later along the same timeline as the M113 APC in the early 1950s.

By the end of the Korean War, most of the Amtracs that had seen service for a decade were in need of repair and upgrading, with many donated to the armed forces of the Philippines and South Korea. In the meantime, the US Marine Corps issued specifications for a fully enclosed amphibious APC in 1947.

The BorgWarner design was chosen and testing was completed by 1952. In time, a gun carrier and air defence variant were built, along with converted command, engineering and recovery vehicles. A total of 1,124 LVTP5s were completed by 1957, while another 210 examples of a design from the rival Food Machinery Corporation were also built.

Considerably larger than its predecessors, the LVTP5 weighed nearly 37½ tons, stretched nearly 30ft in length and resembled a gigantic refrigerator. Its payload capacity was up to six tons in water and nine tons on firm ground. The welded steel hull provided minimal protection for passengers, with maximum thickness just shy of an inch, and the LVTP5 was further recognizable by its two cupolas for the commander and driver, seated forward to the right and left, while a gunner was assigned according to vehicle variant with a single .30-calibre Browning M1919 machine gun. The passenger compartment nearly ran the length of the vehicle and could accommodate up to 34 fully loaded combat troops. Passengers exited forward via doors and a ramp in similar fashion to the larger Landing Ship, Tank (LST). The 704hp Continental LV-1790-1 V-12 petrol engine generated a top land speed of 30mph and water speed of nearly 7mph.

The Marines' 1st and 3rd Amphibian Tractor Battalions were deployed to Vietnam as components of the 1st and 3rd Divisions. Each battalion included up to 20 LVTP5s or other LVTs in troop carrier, command and other modified configurations. Amphibious operations were infrequent in Vietnam, while on land the M113 proved more adept at troop delivery to combat zones and direct fire support.

The LVTP5 often experienced mechanical difficulties and was susceptible to land mines. While the troop carrier was most commonly used, others provided cargo transport and the LVTH-6, mounting a 105mm howitzer, was employed in indirect artillery support. ∎

An LVTP5 is shown in convoy south of the port of Da Nang, South Vietnam, during Operation Oklahoma Hills in 1968. *(US Marine Corps Archives)*

LVTP5 taking part in amphibious exercises in the spring of 1968. *(US Marine Corps)*

CADILLAC GAGE COMMANDO V-100 (M706)

Engineers with the Cadillac Gage division of Terra-Space Company anticipated a future US military requirement for an amphibious, multipurpose vehicle that could fill the roles of armoured personnel carrier (APC), scout and reconnaissance, convoy escort, command and even riot control. Vietnam provided an early proving ground for its V-100 vehicle family, including two prominent derivatives, the V-150 and V-200.

Nicknamed the 'Commando', the new vehicle was designed in 1960. Testing was concluded by 1963 and the proposed production model was sent to Vietnam for field evaluation in the same year. In 1964, the V-100 went into full production with the US Army designation of M706. Since the Army of the Republic of Vietnam (ARVN) was the first recipient of the 'Commando' in the field, for a time US forces 'borrowed' working examples in the mid-1960s until their own were officially procured and placed in action from 1968.

The Commando was affectionately known in Vietnam as the 'Duck' or the 'V' due to its sloped hull. It quickly proved its versatility and was widely deployed with the US Army, Marine Corps, USAF and allied troops. Its primary role had been foreseen as a security vehicle assigned to the US Army's Military Police, but it excelled in multiple settings. The USAF found it useful as a security vehicle guarding against communist insurgent strikes. When an attack occurred, the mobile M706 responded with firepower and mobility.

This retired M706 with Military Police markings is on display at Fort Leonard Wood, Missouri. *(Creative Commons Nevada Tumbleweed (Mark Holloway) via Wikimedia Commons)*

V-150 in service with the Philippine National Police Special Action Force. *(Creative Commons Rhk111 via Wikimedia Commons)*

During the Tet Offensive of 1968, the seven-ton M706 was effective in urban warfare after communist guerrillas assaulted the South Vietnamese capital of Saigon and other cities during weeks of fighting. In the field, the Commando and its three-man crew of commander, gunner and driver could deliver nine fully loaded combat troops to a hot spot.

To maintain economy of production, the 4X4 wheeled vehicle shared numerous components with other vehicles. The axles were similar to the M35 truck series, while the 210hp Chrysler V-8 petrol engine was identical to the powerplant of the M113 APC, producing a top speed of 62mph on the road and 3mph in water. Large tyres were mounted to provide good ground clearance. Steel alloy hull protection of ¼in armour was heavy and effective against small-arms fire and shell fragments, but susceptible to land mines.

The Commando mounted a variety of armament, with the earliest V-100 carrying a pair of M37 Browning .30-calibre machine guns in a fully rotating turret. Some vehicles received .50-calibre Browning M2 machine guns, smoke dischargers and a 40mm grenade launcher. The V-200 variant was built for the export market with an elongated hull, while the V-150 was an integration of the two earlier models with a heavier turret, diverse armament configurations and options for diesel or petrol engines. More than 10,000 vehicles in all variants were built before production halted in 2000 after 36 years. ∎

Two USAF V-100s patrol the perimeter of an air base in Vietnam, 1968. *(US Air Force)*

M35 SERIES CARGO TRUCK

An icon of the US military, the M35 series or 'Deuce and a Half' was deployed widely in Vietnam. *(Creative Commons Steve F-E-Cameron via Wikimedia Commons)*

At the end of World War Two, General Dwight D Eisenhower credited the GMC 2½-ton truck as decisive equipment that helped defeat the Axis powers. The 6X6 cargo truck earned the nickname 'Deuce and a Half' in the process and that name has survived to this day. In Vietnam, an improved version, the M35 2½-ton 6X6 cargo truck, was widely used, with the intention of eventually replacing the GMC CCKW and M135.

In 1949, the REO Motor Car Company began work on a new design for a large cargo carrier and, a year later, the M35 had become the optimal production model, its 10-wheel, dual tandem construction being considered superior to an earlier six-wheel version. Production got underway in 1950 and continued through upgrades and temporary pauses to the end of the 20th Century. Through the years, the M35 series has been manufactured by REO, Kaiser, Studebaker and others, including manufacturers in South Korea and Canada.

Weighing nearly 7½ tons, the M35 stood 9¼ft tall with a length of nearly 23ft and width of 7¾ft. Its original powerplant was the 127hp, six-cylinder REO Gold Comet or Continental OA-331 petrol engine generating a top speed of 58mph and a range of 500 miles. Later variants were fitted with other engines, including diesel conversions. The standard M35 was officially capable of carrying a 5,000lb load in off-road operations or twice that over improved roadways.

The M35A2 variant carried a forward winch for vehicle recovery and extrication from mud or sand. The spacious cargo bed was 8ft wide by 12ft long, and the truck was commonly used to move ammunition, supplies and troops. Canvas soft-tops were readily available, although hard-top versions were sometimes used for cold weather operations. In addition to the cargo configuration, the M35 was also built in construction, wrecker, shop van, command and tanker variants.

Although the M35 did not fully replace the M135 until the mid-1960s, the two served virtually side by side in Vietnam. One of the most effective innovations of the M35 came out of necessity, with the 'gun truck' offering some protection

This M35A2 cargo truck was photographed in 2014 at an antique and classic vehicle show in Rockville, Maryland. *(Creative Commons CZmarlin via Wikimedia Commons)*

The versatile M35 2½-ton cargo truck with a trailer in tow. *(Creative Commons CZmarlin via Wikimedia Commons)*

A Vietnam-era 'gun truck' on display at Fort Eustis, Virginia. *(Creative Commons Yellowute via Wikimedia Commons)*

This M109A2 shop van derived from the 'Deuce and a Half' was outfitted as a workshop on wheels. *(Creative Commons Alf van Beem via Wikimedia Commons)*

Jeeps mounting 7.62mm light machine guns were available for defence and the gap that developed between two sections of the convoy was inviting to the enemy. Suddenly, a Viet Cong 57mm recoilless rifle barked and one of the escorting Jeeps went up in flames. The surrounding area erupted with gunfire along a section of Route 19 stretching more than 750 yards. The slow fuel tanker was set ablaze and, within minutes, three of the convoy's cargo trucks had been raked with machine-gun and rifle fire, disabling them.

A helicopter company of the 1st Cavalry Division was nearby and, when the noise of the ambush reached them, the pilots leaped to their choppers. However, the fighting had subsided by the time help arrived. The Viet Cong had hit hard and then vanished. Still, the Air Cavalry helicopters strrafed the treeline adjacent to the roadway with machine guns and, within the hour, an AC-47 gunship brought added firepower. During the brief firefight, 30 vehicles had been destroyed and 17 Americans had been killed in action and another 17 wounded.

After this, the drivers of the Eighth Transportation Group began carrying rifles and automatic weapons for personal protection, while machine guns and armour were added to any early version of the field-modified 'gun truck'. By mid-1968, heavier weapons had become a familiar sight, although there was no standard arms configuration. Weapons were scrounged from other vehicles or helicopters and installed to provide some ability to fight back during hazardous supply missions. The improvisations undoubtedly reduced the number of US casualties and boosted confidence in the field. When American forces left Southeast Asia, most of the gun trucks were disarmed and reverted to their original cargo state.

Today, the M35 series of medium-duty trucks remain in service with US National Guard and reserve units and the concept of the 'gun truck' is still alive with the armed forces of several nations that have received the 'Deuce and a Half' for their military use. ■

and defence against Viet Cong ambushes when military convoys ventured into the countryside.

As losses were incurred due to enemy attacks, the Americans took the initiative to give their convoys a chance to defend themselves. Conversions to 'gun truck' capabilities were often performed in the field. These included the installation of a quad .50-calibre anti-aircraft gun in the cargo bed or other armaments such as an M60 7.62mm light machine gun, M79 grenade launcher or M134 Minigun that fired from 2,000-6,000 rounds of 7.62mm ammunition per minute. Armour protection was added to some trucks to improve survivability.

One difficult day weighed heavily on the decision to develop the 'gun truck' in Vietnam. On September 2, 1967, the US Eighth Transportation Group sent 39 vehicles down Route 19, an old highway built by the French, to deliver supplies to the 1st Cavalry Division (Airmobile). With the supplies delivered, the trucks set out on the return trek from Pleiku to their base at Qui Nhon. When a fuel tanker slowed the convoy, the commanding officer became worried. Only a pair of M151

Royal Thai Marines come ashore aboard an M35 during exercises with US troops in the 1990s. *(US Government)*

M135 TRUCK

The M135 was the GMC follow-on from its World War Two CCKW 2½-ton truck. *(Creative Commons J Hazard via Wikimedia Commons)*

General Motors (GMC) did not sit idly by when the US Army standardised the post-World War Two REO-built 6X6 M35 2½-ton truck in 1949. After all, it was the GMC CCKW that set the real working standard of excellence during the war and ushered in the famous nickname for this military workhorse, the 'Deuce and a Half'.

When GMC invested its own capital to develop a successor to the CCKW in the early 1950s, the new model shared many components with its predecessor. GMC also had a distinct advantage given the amount of spare parts that were stockpiled in army warehouses across the United States. It appeared that the M135 might take on the leading role, but it was not to be. The M135 was labelled a substitute standard by the US Army and was destined to be produced in far fewer numbers than the M35.

The M135 was still destined to serve alongside its rival in Vietnam, only in fewer numbers and primarily in the earlier years of US involvement. In time, the M135 did become the primary vehicle of its type with the Canadian armed forces, serving for three decades.

The primary change from the original GMC 2 ½-ton truck was the introduction of the company's Hydra-Matic automatic transmission with a rear pump that facilitated pull-starting. The M135 was powered by the straight-six

M135 truck on display at the Aviation Hall of Fame and Museum in New Jersey. *(Creative Commons Ad Meskens via Wikimedia Commons)*

GMC 302 petrol engine, with oversize single tyres for better off-road performance. When the first of the M135s were shipped to Korea in the 1950-1953 conflict, the transmission still needed to have a few bugs ironed out. Most of these were remedied, but the reputation of suboptimal performance lingered. Other changes included a 24-volt electrical system and sealed waterproof ignition.

The M135 cargo bed was mounted low, which allowed combat loaded soldiers to climb aboard and exit the vehicle more easily. A fold-out step was added to the tailgate, while the cargo bed was narrower than that of contemporary dual-wheel trucks. The truck was also equipped with a Gar Wood CA514 10,000lb winch. It weighed just over six tons, stood 8¾ft high, and was nearly 22½ft long.

The M135 remained a 6X6 vehicle with characteristics similar to earlier and contemporary designs. The first rolled off the assembly line on September 13, 1951, and before the run ceased four years later a total of 62,380 had been completed. The M135 was praised for its ruggedness but, according to some sources, it was a target for replacement right along with the CCKW when the new REO M35 became available in quantity.

The M135 was followed in series by the GMC M211. ■

This M217 tanker truck was modified from the GMC M135. *(US Army)*

M54 CARGO TRUCK

The M54 five-ton truck designed by International Harvester was a mainstay of heavy transport in Vietnam. *(US Army)*

This M543 wrecker variant of the M39 series served with the Australian armed forces.
(Creative Commons sv1ambo via Wikimedia Commons)

In the years following World War Two, International Harvester developed a successor to the military heavy trucks built by Mack, Diamond T, White and Brockway. Its M39 series entered production in 1951 and the M54 cargo variant proved the mainstay of the line during the Vietnam conflict.

The 6X6 M54 was designed to carry a five-ton load in all terrains. Its cargo bed stretched 7ft by 14ft and was a low-sided box with a hinged tailgate, side racks and bows stretched overhead for a canvas cover. Seating for combat troops was available as well. The original M54 could not be loaded from the sides, so an improved M54A1C was adapted with drop sides for easier access. When the vehicle was equipped with a winch, it mounted the 20,000lb Garwood type at the front.

After International Harvester initiated production, Kaiser, Mack and Diamond T also produced the M54 in limited numbers. The burly truck was initially powered by the 224hp, six-cylinder, overhead valve inline Continental R6602 petrol engine generating a top speed of 52mph and a range of 280 miles. The A1 variant was upgraded with a 210hp, six-cylinder, turbocharged Mack ENDT diesel, and the A2 incorporated the Continental LDS-465-1A multi-fuel engine.

The M39 series was utilised by all branches of the US armed forces in Vietnam, as well as by the Army of the Republic of Vietnam. Its M54 cargo model was just over 26ft long and nearly 10ft tall. It weighed just shy of 10 tons empty and 15 tons fully loaded.

The M54 was perhaps the most common vehicle in Vietnam to be outfitted as an armoured gun truck for convoy escort. The first of these mounted a pair of M60 7.62mm light machine guns or .50-calibre Browning M2 heavy machine gun. These were mounted in the cargo bed and protection for the gunners came in the form of wooden planks and sandbags, while steel plating was attached to the two-man cab doors and windshield.

Maintenance crews were continually tinkering with the armament of the gun trucks, but they soon became indispensable elements of convoy security. By 1969, at least 100 gun trucks were serving with the eight transport battalions of the US Army in South Vietnam. Tactics were developed with a single gun truck for every 10 cargo-carrying vehicles in a convoy. If contact was made with the enemy, the gun trucks engaged while the others accelerated through the zone of fire.

Along with the M54 cargo variant, the International Harvester M39 line included the M55 long cargo, M543 wrecker, M328A1 bridge transport, M291A1 expansible van, M51 dump truck and M52 tractor. In 1970, the M809 series began replacing the M39s in frontline use. ■

American soldiers man the weapons on this gun truck nicknamed *Glory Stompers*, **December 1969**.
(Creative Commons Hunter, John Philip via Wikimedia Commons)

DODGE **M37**

Conceived as a replacement for the Dodge WC series of trucks that were used across the globe during World War Two, the Dodge M37 was a ¾-ton, four-wheel-drive light duty truck that was engineered during the early days of the Cold War and served with frontline US military units in both Korea and Vietnam.

Six prototypes were evaluated and the first M37 test vehicle was completed in December 1950. The M37 was produced from 1951 to 1968, primarily at the Dodge Truck Assembly Plant in Warren, Michigan, and nearly 116,000 units in various configurations entered service. Production geared up in January 1951, with 11,000 vehicles produced in that year alone. As customary, the M37 shared numerous components and features with its predecessor, while a modernisation of some aspects improved performance and utility, such as the installation of a pickup truck bed rather than the earlier WC series platform.

The powerplant of the M37 was a 1930s passenger car engine and holdover from the WC series. The 78hp straight-six Dodge T-245 produced a top speed of 55mph and a range of 225 miles. With ample ground clearance, the truck was 7½ft high and nearly 16ft long. Its performance was robust and its mechanics were simple, making for easy maintenance. Capable of negotiating difficult terrain, it delivered a substantial payload for its size.

Modifications to the original M37 began in 1958, with the new variants designated

Dodge M37 light duty truck at an airshow in the UK in 2009. *(Creative Commons Dave Hitchborne via Wikimedia Commons)*

the M37B1, with a total of 47,600 being constructed through the end of production. Concurrently, about 4,500 Canadian versions of the truck were built between 1951 and 1955 and known as the M37CDN. The truck was produced in command variants as the M42, telephone maintenance types as the V41, enclosed utility vehicles as the M152, along with the M43 ambulance and the R2 in field fire service. Altogether at least 11 variants and subvariants were built.

As the M37s in service began to age, engine issues emerged, exacerbated by the regularly higher road speeds with a vehicle designed primarily to transport heavy loads. The low gear ratio of the powerplant had been intended mainly for heavy hauling.

The M37's intended replacement, the Kaiser Jeep M715, did not fare well in the field, thus the Dodge M880 became the primary successor to the M37 by the 1970s. After the truck was retired from military service, it remained active with US government agencies and many were sold direct to the public or disposed of at auction as surplus. ∎

Dodge M37 in the American West, probably during a period of nuclear testing. *(National Nuclear Security Administration Nevada Site Office)*

A standard canvas cover deployed over the bed of a Dodge M37. *(Creative Commons SG2012 via Wikimedia Commons)*

KAISER JEEP **M715**

The Kaiser Jeep M715 was the first US military M-series vehicle to be constructed primarily from commercially available components. The rugged reputation of the Jeep was already established and stretched back to World War Two, when Willys-Overland had received the primary contract to produce the Jeep for the Allies. By 1953, Willys-Overland had experienced economic difficulties and been sold to Kaiser Motors.

Kaiser dedicated its operations to producing vehicles under the Jeep name and ceased production of passenger cars. By the mid-1960s, the company had undertaken design and development of a light truck to replace the standard US Army Dodge M37. Work began in 1965 and the vehicle entered production in 1967. As many as 33,000 were completed at the company's assembly plant in Toledo, Ohio, during a run that ended in 1969. The M715 saw service in Vietnam and with US forces in South Korea and across NATO bases in Europe.

The M715 was often referred to as the 'Five Quarter' due to its 1¼-ton cargo capacity. Its straight-six Jeep Tornado overhead cam petrol engine generated 140hp and a top speed of 55mph. The base M715 served as a cargo carrier and troop transport, while variants were employed as maintenance and utility (M724), ambulance (M725) and telephone maintenance (M726) vehicles. The truck weighed nearly 4½ tons fully loaded, stood nearly 8½ft high at bed level and was often equipped with a winch on the front bumper to extricate other vehicles mired in mud, sand or swamps.

For all its perceived potential, the M715 proved a disappointment in the field. Its overhead cam engine was unreliable due to issues with maintenance and was inherently underpowered for the jobs intended, unlike the Dodge M37 it was built to replace. The engine was also known to consume excessive amounts of oil and was dropped from Kaiser civilian production vehicles by 1968. Further, the winch sometimes failed when its driveshaft separated, in turn disrupting the steering and potentially causing

A Kaiser Jeep M715 light truck on display with other vehicles. *(Creative Commons Mr.choppers via Wikimedia Commons)*

Photo of the Kaiser Jeep M715 from the operator's manual. *(United States Government)*

the driver to lose control. Weaknesses were discovered in some of the M715 frames, many of which had been sent to Korea, and these were repaired by a contracted company in Korea while the vehicles were inactive at motor depots. Beginning in 1976, the Dodge M880 series began replacing the M715 with US military forces.

Despite its inauspicious military career, the M715 has become a popular vehicle with collectors. A similar design is also in production by Kia, which has contracted with the South Korean Army to produce its KM450 under US government license. Other M715-related vehicle types are also being evaluated and AM General, the successor to Kaiser, produced an updated version called the AM 715 in the late 1970s. ■

The Kaiser Jeep M715 was plagued with mechanical issues and underpowered for the jobs intended in Vietnam and elsewhere. *(Creative Commons JTOcchialini via Wikimedia Commons)*

M76 OTTER

Designed and manufactured by the Pontiac Motor Division of General Motors, the M76 Otter was intended as a replacement for the M29 Weasel amphibious cargo carrier that had seen service during World War Two. Design work began in the late 1940s and the prototype was designated the T46. Although both the US Army and the US Marine Corps showed early interest in the project, the army withdrew, leaving the Marines to receive the first production M76s, which entered service in the early 1950s and were later utilised extensively in Vietnam.

The M76 was constructed of aluminium and powered by a 130hp, four-cylinder Continental AIO-268 – originally an aircraft engine - generating a land speed of 30mph. As with the M56 Scorpion anti-tank vehicle, the Otter was fully tracked in combination with pneumatic road wheels. This assembly lightened the overall weight of the M76 and provided good mobility in mud, swamp and sand. A large propeller was used to negotiate waterways, with steering in water accomplished by manipulating the tracks; when not in use, the propeller was folded upward. The Otter could also function as an ambulance and in a recovery role by utilising its towing hook and chain to pull wheeled vehicles free from mud or difficult terrain.

The driver sat on the left with an open passenger seat to the right, steering the vehicle with tillers that resembled the handlebars of a bicycle; the two seats were separated by the housing for the propeller driveshaft. The fully enclosed cargo area could transport eight fully loaded combat Marines or 3,000lb of supplies, and hatches were installed in the ceiling. The only defensive armament aboard the M76 was a Browning M2 .50-calibre machine gun mounted outside a hatch over the passenger seat. The vehicle was entered via conventional doors for the driver and forward passenger, while a rear door allowed ingress and egress for troops and cargo.

Since the M76 was unarmoured, it was susceptible to enemy small-arms fire, so field modifications were sometimes added to provide more protection. On occasion, Marines installed armour sheeting over cabin windows and around the .50-calibre machine gun position.

The first 33 Otters arrived in Vietnam in 1965 and were placed with the 3rd Motor Transport Battalion, 1st Marine Brigade, 1st Marine Division Fleet Logistics Support Command at Da Nang. The most notable deployment of the M76 took place during the battle of Dong Ha in Quang Tri Province from April 30 to May 3, 1968. The Otter crews performed with great heroism and efficiency, with Captain Jay R Vargas of Company G, 2nd Battalion, 4th Marines, 9th Amphibious Brigade, receiving the Medal of Honor for heroism during the fighting.

Replaced by the M116 Husky in the primary amphibious transport role, the Otter remained active with Marine Corps service and supply units until the 1970s. ■

An M76 Otter amphibious transport vehicle traverses soggy terrain in Vietnam. *(US Department of Defense Marine Corps photo)*

An M76 Otter at a US Marines command post in Vietnam, 1966. *(Creative Commons Archives Branch, USMC History Division via Wikimedia Commons)*

A Marine sits ready at the .50-calibre machine gun position atop an M76 Otter. *(US Department of Defense Marine Corps photo)*

M116 HUSKY

In the early 1960s, the Pacific Car and Foundry Company (PCFC) began design work on an amphibious vehicle to replace the M76 Otter in service with the US Marine Corps. The result was the M116 Husky. Although PCFC completed four prototypes and three pre-production examples and entered a bid for the full production run, the contract was awarded to Blaw-Knox. Only 197 M116s were built, but the vehicle is remembered for its service in Vietnam.

Powered by a Chevrolet V-8, the Husky was capable of a top speed of 37mph on land and 4mph in water. Designed for movement in marginal terrain, including streams, marshes and beaches, the fully tracked vehicle did not require a water propulsion system as the movement of the tracks was sufficient in each environment. With a height of only 6ft, 9in and width of 6ft, 8in, the M116 was a rather compact vehicle with a low silhouette.

The Husky entered service with the Marines in the spring of 1969 with the 11th Motor Transport Battalion, 1st Marine Division, operating in the vicinity of the coastal port of Da Nang. In practice, it did somewhat reduce Marine dependence on helicopter-borne resupply efforts.

The M116 chassis was constructed of aluminium and unarmoured, contributing to its light weight of 10,600lb, low ground pressure and ease of mobility. It carried a payload of up to 3,000lb, either supplies or up to 13 passengers. However,

The M733 was an armed and armoured transport vehicle that served as an escort in Vietnam. This example served with the armed forces of Taiwan. *(Creative Commons 玄史生 via Wikimedia Commons)*

when the Husky ventured into hostile territory it was quite vulnerable.

This limitation was illustrated by the loss of an M116 on a supply mission in October 1969. Several Huskies had set out to deliver supplies and ammunition to a Marine outpost near the

US Marines of the 11th Motor Transport Battalion load harvested rice onto an M116 Husky, March 14, 1970. *(National Archives and Records Administration official Marine Corps photo)*

South Vietnamese border with neighbouring Laos. The Huskies reached their objective without incident, but during the return trek one of them struck a Soviet-made box mine buried in the dirt roadway by Viet Cong guerrillas. All four Marines aboard were killed in the blast.

To minimise the risk of losses to enemy action, steel plating capable of withstanding .30-calibre rounds and extensive armament were added to some Huskies. Designated the M733, PCFC built 93 of them, with the first delivered to the Marine Corps in 1966. They were placed in service in Vietnam in August 1969 to provide convoy escort to the M116 and armed with one or more 7.62mm M60 light machine guns, an 81mm mortar and, at times, a Browning M2 .50-calibre machine gun. ■

M116 Huskies carrying Vietnamese farmers across a flooded field. *(National Archives and Records Administration official Marine Corps photo)*

M548 CARGO CARRIER

The M548 Cargo Carrier was adapted from the M113 APC as an ammunition carrier. *(Creative Commons Glunggenbauer via Wikimedia Commons)*

An artillery shell hangs from a winch at the rear of an M548. *(Creative Commons Hornet Driver via Wikimedia Commons)*

As a derivative of the M113 Armored Personnel Carrier (APC), the longevity of the M548 Cargo Carrier should come as no surprise. Stretching the applications of the M113 led to a variety of uses in the widening mechanisation requirements of the US armed forces.

Adaptations were frequent in the 1950s and the M548 had been mocked up, tested and approved for production by 1964. Like its parent, the M548 was manufactured by Food Machinery and Chemical Corporation (FMC) of California, and it was later built by the Spanish contractor Oto Melara under license.

The M548 was built to haul cargo, particularly artillery ammunition for the 155mm Paladin self-propelled howitzer, the M107 275mm self-propelled gun, the M110 8in howitzer and the crewmen required to operate these weapons. It featured a spacious rear cargo bed that was accessed by a wide door and could accommodate a payload of six tons.

The M548 resulted from a US Army Signal Corps specification for a fully tracked vehicle to carry its AN/MPQ-32 counterbattery radar apparatus. One of the prototypes delivered by FMC was the XM548. Although the radar was deemed too heavy for the vehicle, the Army Material Command Technical Committee had distributed a requirement for a fully tracked cargo carrier in the spring of 1964. Opportunity led to the adoption of the modified M113A1 as the XM548E1 and, ultimately, the M548.

In short order, the M548 became the prime tracked cargo carrier of the US Army. The vehicle also served as the platform for further derivatives such as the M752 launcher for the Lancer tactical surface-to-surface missile, its M688 loader/transporter and the basis for the mobile M730 Chaparral surface-to-air missile. The M548 was also well-suited to radio, communications, electronics and command configurations.

In Vietnam, the M548 displayed an aptitude for the cargo transport and other roles in the varied climatic and terrain conditions of Southeast Asia. The vehicle was unarmoured and weighed just over 14 tons with a standard crew of four, mounted a single .50-calibre Browning M2 heavy machine gun for air and ground defence and provided a clearance at the rear of more than nine feet to facilitate loading and unloading of cargo. The M548 was over 19ft long and nearly 10ft wide. Its cab was fully enclosed.

Powered by the 204hp, six-cylinder Detroit Diesel 6V53 engine, the M548 was capable of a top road speed of 38mph, while offroad operations were sometimes challenging due to the necessity of keeping the track tension constant. The M548 has been upgraded several times since entering service in the early 1960s and remains active with numerous countries. ∎

An M548 modified to mount a Quad .50-calibre anti-aircraft machine gun, Vietnam, February 1968. *(US Army)*

M520 GOER

Officially named the M520 Truck, Cargo, 8-ton, 4X4, in Vietnam the M520 earned the nickname 'Goer' (Go-ability with Overall Economy and Reliability). This came about because it delivered time and again, going where other trucks and transport vehicles could not venture. Even before production of the vehicle was approved, it was being field tested in Germany and Vietnam in 1966. The 'Goer' was in demand soon after its pre-production deployment to Southeast Asia, and its 90% availability rate was testament to its rugged construction, particularly since ample replacement parts were not available until 1972.

During the mid-1950s, the US Army's requirement for a new tactical truck that could go offroad in the most difficult terrain and provide a more robust payload than existing transport led to a trio of development contracts being issued to the Caterpillar Tractor Company, Clark Equipment and Le Tourneau-Westinghouse. Caterpillar received a contract for eight prototype vehicles in 1960, and these were delivered over the next two years in 8-ton cargo and 10-ton wrecker and tanker configurations. Twenty-three more were ordered in 1963 for the field testing phase.

Sources indicate that the M520 was designed and manufactured by Pacific Car and Foundry Company or designed by Caterpillar and built by Marinette Marine of Wisconsin. Interestingly, the Caterpillar contract for full production apparently was not received from the US government until 1971. From then, 812 M520 standard cargo examples were completed, while 371 M559 tankers and 117 M553 wreckers were built during the production run from 1972 to 1976. At times, the M520 was fitted with a crane and designated the M877.

Powered by diesel engines, first the Caterpillar D333 multifuel and then the diesel Caterpillar D333C, the vehicle was capable of 35mph. Its dimensions were 8ft high, 9ft wide and

This M520 'Goer' is shown in its element, churning through mud to make a delivery. *(US Army)*

M520 'Goer' on a dirt road during exercises in the 1980s. *(US Army)*

Demonstrating its amphibious qualities and articulation, this M520 carries a full load of cargo. *(US Army)*

32ft long, allowing the M520 to negotiate narrow spaces. It weighed 13½ tons and was fully amphibious. The front-mounted engine and hydraulic system were key components of its agility in difficult terrain, delivering substantial cargo to units deployed in remote mountainous or swamp areas. It was articulated to improve manoeuvrability.

The 'Goer' was designed with a tailgate and side doors that dropped to facilitate the rapid loading and unloading of cargo. The vehicle was four-wheel-drive offroad, but reverted to front-wheel-drive on tarmac. At times, the vehicle had a tendency to bounce considerably at top road speed, for which the driver compensated by swaying the wheel left and right while in motion.

By the 1980s, the M520 was being phased out in favour of the Oshkosh Heavy Expanded Mobility Tactical Truck series. ■

M561 GAMA GOAT

The articulation feature of the M561 'Gama Goat' is visible in this photo taken during exercises. *(US Department of Defense)*

Reports from the French military during its involvement in Vietnam indicated that reliable cargo and troop transport was a necessity, but that existing vehicles were inadequate. In response, the US Defense Department's Advanced Research Projects Agency authorised a research initiative dubbed Agile for a new tactical truck.

By 1959, when the government effort began, inventor and engineer Roger Gamaunt had already been working for more than a decade on an articulated body for such a vehicle involving three axles. In the same year, Chance Vought began developing a truck that incorporated Gamaunt's system. Prototype work proceeded with Gamaunt as a contract partner with Chance Vought. Eventually, Ling-Temco-Vought Aerospace won the competition for the new vehicle, already dubbed the 'Gama Goat', for production at its Consolidated Diesel Electric Company in Charlotte, North Carolina. Production was undertaken in the spring of 1968, with a three-year contract issued to produce vehicles for both the US Army and Marine Corps. When the run ended, a total of 15,274 M561s had been built.

The first production M561s arrived in South Vietnam in 1969, and the 'Gama Goat' nickname was widely used to acknowledge Gamaunt as the inventor of the articulating feature and the ability of the vehicle to negotiate difficult terrain with the surefooted performance of a mountain goat.

Although the M561 offered an improvement over previous cargo and troop transport vehicles, drawbacks were discovered in the field. The 101hp, three-cylinder Detroit Diesel 3-53 engine that delivered a top road speed of 59mphr proved unable to handle terrain that included mud, water and clinging vines, which was frequently the case in Vietnam. Reports of mechanical breakdowns reached alarming numbers. A compilation of issues with 566 vehicles in repair shops in Vietnam included failures with transmissions, brake cylinders and O-ring seals. The rigours of the field only magnified these maintenance concerns.

The M561 did feature improved manoeuvrability with its articulation feature. It weighed just over 3½ tons, was nearly 8ft tall and 12ft wide. Its wide cargo bay could be covered with a tarpaulin as needed, and it was designed to be airmobile via parachute. However, in the field, it was determined that the buoyancy of the M561 was overrated, and drivers were required to take on additional training to navigate waterways. Although its offroad characteristics were admirable, its road handling was difficult, challenging drivers to maintain control.

By 1973, the 'Gama Goat' was regularly being relegated to reserve status. It was fully supplanted in the 1980s by the Humvee and the last of the M561s to see action were deployed in Grenada with the US Marines in 1983. ■

This 'Gama Goat' prototype is shown negotiating rugged terrain during trials in 1965. *(US Department of Defense)*

M561 towing an artillery piece during training in the 1980s. *(US Department of Defense)*

10-Ton 6x6 Truck Tractor M123 - Left Front View

The M123 10-ton truck was designed and built by Mack from the 1950s. *(US Army)*

10-Ton 6x6 Truck, Cargo M125 - Left Front View

M125 10-ton truck with the single winch at the front bumper. Note the ribs above the cargo area to accommodate a canvas cover. *(US Army)*

M123/125 10-TON TRUCK

When the US Army issued specifications for a replacement for the World War Two-vintage Mack NO series of heavy duty trucks, Mack stepped up again to design a family of trucks that provided the brawn for the heaviest of transport requirements.

While the M123 was used to tow heavy trailers, many of them flatbeds carrying main battle tanks, the M125 was a heavy cargo transport and prime mover that was capable of towing 155mm howitzers and 203mm artillery pieces. The two effectively filled the requirements of the 1949 directive, with Mack constructing 392 M123s and 552 M125s from 1955 to 1958. Various upgrades and modifications occurred through 1969, and Consolidated Diesel Electric Company joined the manufacturing effort in 1965 to build 3,188 diesel-powered M123A variants. In the same year, Mack converted petrol M123s to diesel engines.

Both the M123 and M125 were six-wheel-drive. They were deployed to Vietnam to provide heavy transport, with the US Marine Corps and other allied countries also accepting the types into service. The trucks weighed more than 16 tons empty and stood more than 9ft high. They were over 23ft long and 9½ft wide. Mack held over the drivetrain from the previous NO series, while trucks built in the 1950s were powered by the 297hp petrol V8 LeRoi T-H844 engine, delivering a top speed of 42mph. By the 1960s, the 300hp Cummins V8 diesel engines were introduced with the M123.

The M123 was intended to haul M15A2 semi trailer with a higher load plate and coupling pin than early standard trailers. It was built with twin winches and a high mounted fifth wheel above its frame rails, but this was reduced to a lower fifth wheel with the M123C and as other trailers were introduced. The cab design was shared with the lighter trucks in military service, with either a removable canvas roof or fitted hard roof. It appeared larger than the other cabs due to the scaling for the size of the overall vehicle.

The M125 had a spacious cargo bed and sides that folded down to facilitate easy loading and unloading. The trailer was 14ft long, with folding seats for troop transport. Canvas covers were available to protect cargo during inclement weather. A single winch was mounted on the front bumper and a chain hoist was attached at the rear for ammunition loading.

The M123 remained in service with the US Army into the 1990s, while the M125 saw less use by the 1980s due to the US Army's move toward self-propelled artillery. ■

This M123/M125 10-ton truck is shown with an M110 203mm howitzer aboard its trailer. *(US Department of Defense)*

CATERPILLAR D7E BULLDOZER

A D7E bulldozer and Rome Plow cuts down a tree in the Vietnamese jungle. *(US Army)*

Mounting the Rome Plow kit in September 1967, Caterpillar D7Es take on the Vietnamese jungle. *(US Army Corps of Engineers)*

The first Caterpillar D7 bulldozer was manufactured in 1938, and three decades later the heavy mover was engaged in its third military action with the D7E, which entered production in 1961. From the 1930s to the present, the iconic bulldozer line has maintained its place among critical machines of the US military.

The basic D7 bulldozer weighed just under 16 tons, stood 8ft high and was just over 8ft wide. It earned a reputation as a splendid earth mover during World War Two and in Korea prior to reaching Vietnam. The D7E was used in the construction of forward bases, airfields, landing zones, residential areas and just about any other task that required earth moving.

In Vietnam it was put to another task that was intended to directly impact the course of the war. The dense jungle provided a haven for Viet Cong guerrillas and one method of depriving the enemy of that deep cover was the removal of it from the landscape. Enter the D7E and its partner, the stinger blade that turned the D7E into a land clearing behemoth. The combined D7E and stinger were referred to as a Rome Plow in reference to the city of Rome, Georgia, north of Atlanta, where the blades were made by the Rome Plow Company.

The use of Agent Orange defoliant did an adequate job in killing jungle canopy, but the jungle floor remained deeply covered with trees and roots, so the solution was to equip the standard US Army tractor with the Rome Plow kit. The plow itself weighed 2½ tons and its stinger at the left-hand edge was designed specifically to cut down trees. The blade was angled at 30° in order to toss cut vegetation to the right. A canopy was installed to protect the bulldozer operator.

The first Rome Plows arrived in South Vietnam in 1967 and it was quickly determined that many combinations of the D7E and the kit would be required to accomplish the quantity of jungle removal necessary. The 59th, 60th, 501st, 538th, 687th and 984th Engineer Companies were assigned the Rome Plow during the course of the war and given the designation as 'land clearing'. A single land clearing company would work for about 45 days before fatigue and maintenance requirements necessitated a rest.

Over the course of the conflict, the US Army cleared 300,000 acres of Vietnamese jungle. One combat officer praised the work of the men who operated the Rome Plow: "For every operation I conduct in an area not cleared, I lose 10 men, as opposed to only one man in an area you've cleared.". ■

A row of Rome Plows parked across from living quarters at Firebase Jerre, South Vietnam, in December 1969. *(US Army)*

M151 JEEP UTILITY TRUCK

Perhaps no other land vehicle of the 20th Century is more closely associated with the US military than the ubiquitous Jeep. By late 1940, engineers at the Bantam Car Company were building the prototype that was accepted into service with the US Army in 1941, after Willys-Overland and The Ford Motor Company participated in early development and the Willys MB design was put into production.

During World War Two, the Jeep was everywhere the US and Allied land forces were, from Pacific islands to the Asian continent, North Africa and Europe. By 1945, more than 630,000 had been built and the sturdy vehicle had become a legendary workhorse. In the early years of the Cold War, Willys produced the M38 series, which made improvements to the original design. Along with World War Two-vintage Jeeps, the M38 served in the Korean War and more than 160,000 were produced in the base vehicle and M38A1 variant.

The US Army continually sought to improve its standard four-wheel-drive utility vehicle and, by 1951, Ford was awarded a contract based on specifications from the Army Ordnance Tank Automotive Command to produce the Truck, Utility, ¼-Ton, 4X4, designated the M151. The new Jeep replaced the M38 series and included a better suspension system with coil springs, although much of the preceding M38's physical dimensions and layout were retained. The new suspension enhanced

The front of the M151 series featured horizontal grill slats rather than the earlier vertical type, but retained the inset headlights. *(US Army)*

cross-country travel at higher speeds and reduced the discomfort of a bumpy ride. The revised M151 also incorporated an integrated unibody structure and eliminated a separate frame, to give slightly more ground clearance. Its 85-inch wheelbase was four inches wider than the M38 and gave the M151 slightly more room in the crew space without adding weight.

The M151 was also nicknamed 'MUTT' (Military Utility Tactical Truck) and, true to its lineage, became a common sight in Vietnam. Many variants were produced, including armed and unarmed vehicles that were used in reconnaissance, command, and transport situations, as well as in the evacuation and ambulance roles. At least 16 iterations of the M151 emerged, some of them mounting an 106mm recoilless rifle, TOW anti-tank missile or .50-calibre Browning M2 machine gun in the rear section. Other variants included the US Marine M1051 firefighter, MRC108 forward air control and FAV Mk I Marine

The M151A2 incorporated improved suspension. *(Creative Commons AlfvanBeem via Wikimedia Commons)*

This M151A2 in US Army livery is shown with a canvas covering. *(US Army)*

An M151A2 fires a TOW anti-tank missile from its mobile mount. *(US Army)*

'Super Jeep', as well as Air Force and Airborne or Ranger fast attack vehicles. The airborne M151 was small enough to fit inside a CH-47 Chinook or CH-53 Sea Stallion helicopter.

Performance was improved substantially when the M151 was powered by the 71hp, four-cylinder Ordnance Continental inline petrol engine, which generated a top road speed of 65mph. Although the vehicle's grille was built with horizontal slats rather than the traditional vertical configuration, Ford engineers continued the Jeep's classic look with rounded head lamps integral to the front of the vehicle. The driver was positioned in front to the left, while a co-driver was seated to the right and passengers were accommodated on bench seating. The vehicle could also carry cargo when necessary. The M151 weighed 1.2 tons, stretched slightly longer than 11ft, and was more than 5ft wide.

Officially replacing the last of the M38A1s still in service, the M151 began rolling off assembly lines in 1960, and Kaiser Jeep, which had acquired Willys-Overland, joined Ford in production. By 1964, the M151A1 incorporated suspension improvements for heavier loads and turn signals on the front fenders. Tests and service-related incidents revealed an exaggerated tendency to roll over, so steps were taken to address the issue with redesigned rear suspension and the installing of a roll bar. The new M151A2 became the production model in 1968. The basic M151

and M151A2 remained in production through 1982, and more than 100,000 were built.

In the field, the US Army found the M151 to be a functional and all-around fine vehicle. However, it was difficult for some drivers to master because steering became an issue at high speed, particularly when cornering or covering rough ground. The Jeep handled better with weight in the rear section, so ammunition boxes filled with sand were sometimes placed there. Still, the M151 was limited to military service as its troublesome suspension caused the Department of Defense to issue a directive that the vehicle was "unsafe for

public highway use" due to liability concerns even after the improvements made in the M151A2.

Despite its drawbacks, the M151 turned in a performance in Vietnam that was worthy of its storied heritage. Variants of the original light truck have served with the armed forces of at least 15 NATO countries and more than 100 countries across the globe. By the late 1980s, the long-serving M151 family was being phased out of primary and secondary use with the US military as the High Mobility Multipurpose Wheeled Vehicle, better known as the Humvee, came into service. ■

This M151A1C mounted a 106mm recoilless rifle in the rear passenger compartment. *(Creative Commons AlfvanBeem via Wikimedia Commons)*

Officers of the US Army's 1st Cavalry Division (Airmobile) attend a briefing with the hood of an M151 as a tabletop, Bong Son, South Vietnam, January 25, 1966. *(US Army)*

M606 JEEP

While this M606 Jeep is shown in US livery, the post-war variant was produced mainly for the export market. *(Creative Commons JoachimKohler-HB via Wikimedia Commons)*

From World War Two through the present day, the Jeep's contribution to the US military and allied forces is unsurpassed by any other vehicle. Through the years with numerous manufacturers, it has maintained a following and its decades of steadfast service have made Jeeps a favourite among collectors.

During the early years of the Cold War, Willys and then Kaiser Jeep continued to supply vehicles to the US military. In 1950, the first post-war Jeep redesign was introduced and became the M38 series. Based on the CJ-3A, which was offered to the public for purchase beginning in 1949, the military M38 series was upgraded in 1953 to the M38A1, featuring a new rounded fender that was needed to accommodate the economical overhead valve, as well as a 75hp, four-cylinder F4-134 Hurricane petrol engine, which produced a top speed of 55mph and range of 75 road miles.

While the company would offer the new engine in its CJ-5 by 1955, an earlier military model was introduced with the same high-fendered look and the less expensive Hurricane F4-134 overhead valve engine. Essentially, the new CJ-3B body style was a CJ-3A with a taller hood. The military version of the CJ-3B was designated the M606. Its features differed from the civilian model, including heavier springs, oversize tyres, blackout lighting and a trailer hitch.

The 4X4 M606 was manufactured from 1953 to 1968 and was offered to the export market during the period of US military aid packages aimed at stemming the spread of communism in Europe and Southeast Asia, particularly the Mutual Defense Assistance Program of 1949 that sent roughly $3 billion in military aid to allied nations. Those examples manufactured by Kaiser Jeep were labelled M606A2 and M606A3. The M606 was not regularly used by the US military, although some examples did find their way into service as security vehicles. Also, US purchases did not include the fender mounted blackout lighting in every case.

The M606 served in Vietnam the Army of the Republic of Vietnam throughto the end of the conflict in 1975, while many examples were also sent to Central and South America. The M606 weighed slightly more than 12 tons, carried a maximum load of nine tons and performed scouting, command and security tasks primarily. In the end, the general purpose Jeep was quite similar to the commercially marketed CJ-5, as well as the CJ-3b, and there is no doubt that its military association, along with its rugged performance reputation, helped to fuel sales to the US public and solidify the classic Jeep as a military icon of 20th Century. ■

This M606 ambulance variant is shown with US Marines in action during the 1960s. *(US Marine Corps)*

This restored 1955 CJ-3B was built in Japan by Mitsubishi under license. *(Creative Commons Mitsupicture via Wikimedia Commons)*

M274 UTILITY PLATFORM TRUCK

The M274 ½-ton 4X4 Utility Platform Truck was not built for aesthetics, but for hard use and presented a look that only a soldier could love. It was nicknamed the 'Mechanical Mule', 'Military Mule' or simply the 'Mule'.

Intended as a light weapon and troop carrier with airborne and infantry at the battalion level, the M274 was introduced in 1956 to supplement the other weapons carriers then in service with the US Army. Willys-Overland had designed a similar vehicle

The M274 Military Mule was completely open. *(US Army Transportation Museum)*

US Marines operate an M274, mounting a 106mm recoilless rifle in rough terrain in Vietnam. *(US Marine Corps Archives)*

An M274 with a Bell UH-1 helicopter during operations in Vietnam in July 1966. *(National Archives and Records Administration)*

near the end of World War Two, but when the M274 was accepted into service, some improvements to the original design had been completed. Basic requirements included a vehicle weight of 750lb or less and a payload capacity of 1,000lb. The original Willys 1950s prototypes could carry 850lb and were built in two-wheel- and four-wheel-drive.

An original patent was applied for in December 1944 and testing took place under US Army control at Eglin Airfield, Florida, through 1948, after which an order was placed for a few vehicles to test as a 'Jungle Burden Carrier'. Production of the M274 was finally inaugurated in 1956, and 11,240 were completed until 1970. The 'Mule' served throughout US involvement in Vietnam, carrying troops and light cargo. If necessary, seating could be removed to accommodate a larger cargo load. Although it was rugged and could traverse difficult terrain, the M274 was completely open, offering little or no protection for driver or passenger, thus was often used in areas deemed clear of enemy activity.

The 16hp, four-cylinder Willys AO4-4-53 engine produced a top speed of 25mph and a range of 108 miles, while later variants received a Continental-Hercules two-cylinder powerplant. The vehicle was just over 4ft high, 4ft wide and shy of 10ft long. A variety of armaments were mounted on the M274's light frame, including the TOW anti-tank missile, M40 106mm recoilless rifle, .50-calibre Browning M2 heavy machine gun and the M60 7.62mm NATO light machine gun. In the event the M274 came under enemy fire, the steering column could be lowered to provide cover for the driver, who could continue to operate the vehicle from a crouched position.

The M274 was active with the US Army into the 1980s, when the Humvee was introduced. However, when it was determined that the Humvee was not well suited to some of the tasks previously assigned to the 'Mule', the Army adopted the John Deer M-Gator, a military adaptation of the civilian Gator utility vehicle. ∎

M578 LIGHT ARMORED RECOVERY VEHICLE

Inevitably, tracked or wheeled armoured vehicles in wartime tned to get disabled or damaged by land mines, enemy fire or mechanical issues. Such was the case in Vietnam. To facilitate repair, the Cold War-era M578 Light Armored Recovery Vehicle (LARV) was available by the time US forces were committed to Southeast Asia in substantial numbers.

The M109 Paladin 155mm self-propelled howitzer and M113 armoured personnel carrier (APC) were commonly deployed to Vietnam, as were the M107 175mm self-propelled gun and M110 203mm (8-inch) self-propelled howitzer. When the need arose, the M578 was robust enough to handle the recovery of these weapons, utilising its crane or heavier forward winch to take control of the immobile vehicle.

Based on the same chassis as the self-propelled M107 and M110, the M578

M578 in the Royal Canadian Ordnance Corps Museum, Montreal, Quebec. *(Creative Commons Skaarup. HA via Wikimedia Commons)*

The rusted hulk of this M578 is on display at Dong Ha, Quang Tri Province, Vietnam. *(Creative Commons Cdvchelsea via Wikimedia Commons)*

An M578 in Vietnam deploys its crane to recover a disabled M551 Sheridan light tank. *(US Army)*

continued in the pattern of the 1956 Pacific Car & Foundry Company's design and progressed through the prototype T120, with the T120E1 entering production with the Food Machinery and Chemical Corporation in 1962. Production continued to the end of the decade, paused then resumed in 1975 with Bowen-McLaughlin-York. The M578 was powered by the Detroit Diesel 345hp, eight-cylinder 8V71T engine, producing a top speed of 37mph and a range of 450 miles. The vehicle weighed 26½ tons, stood 8½ft high, and was just over 10ft wide.

The crew of three included a driver, rigger and an operator for the 360° traversing cab, which utilised a powered crane with a winch capacity of 15 tons. A second winch for dragging was mounted on the front of the cab, with a hefty capacity of 30 tons. These were powered by an onboard generator that could operate when the vehicle was turned off,. The official recovery capacity was listed at 27 tons.

Access to the cab was provided by single doors on each side and double doors at the rear. The operators' field of vision was through a pair of cupolas in the roof of the cab. When the M578 was required to work at night, a spotlight was fitted to the crane boom and headlights were used.

The ½in steel cab provided only limited protection against small-arms fire or shell fragments, and though enemy contact was supposed to be unlikely, a single .50-calibre Browning M2 machine gun was mounted to the turret for defence against opposing aircraft or close infantry.

Production of the M578 ended in 1981 and it was deployed to the Middle East during the 1991 Gulf War. The vehicle has remained in service with many countries for years. ∎

LAND ROVER

Australian Land Rovers roll forward with a convoy in Vietnam in October 1971. *(Creative Commons Ford, John Alfred via Wikimedia Commons)*

he famous British-designed Land Rover served with Australian troops in Vietnam in several roles, including communications, scouting and reconnaissance, medical evacuation and supply and logistics.

The Land Rover Series 1 made its debut at an auto show in Amsterdam, The Netherlands, on April 30, 1948, and was developed primarily by brothers Maurice and Spencer Wilks as an all-terrain vehicle to assist in farm chores. The natural progression to military applications followed with the Series 2 and 2A. The Australian Army received its first Series 1 in 1948 as a replacement for earlier Jeeps and other vehicle types used in World War Two, while the Series 2 was procured in 1958 and the 2A in 1963.

Vietnam-era Land Rovers were powered by 2.3-litre petrol engines that delivered 77hp, a top speed of 50-62mph and a range of 249 miles. The vehicles were fielded in both short and long wheelbases, and 69 were modified to carry the US-made M40 106mm recoilless rifle on a pintle mount between the front seats. These armed Land Rovers were strengthened with a heavier chassis to support the weight of the M40, while the windshield was modified with a split pair of screens to allow the gun to be carried in the locked position pointing forward. The upgraded Land Rovers weighed roughly 1.65 tons and carried a crew of four, including a commander, gunner, loader and driver. After completing trials in 1962, the Series 2 entered service on February 11, 1964, followed by the 2A on July 8, 1966. By the spring of 1969, there were 55 in service with the Australian task force in Vietnam. The vehicle was air transportable by CH-47 Chinook helicopter or Lockheed C130 Hercules and de Havilland DHC-4 Caribou cargo aircraft.

Land Rovers armed with the recoilless rifle were nicknamed 'gun buggies' and saw extensive service in the light mobile ground support role. Since there was virtually no protection from enemy return fire, they usually employed the 'shoot and scoot' tactic, displacing immediately after their own weapon was fired to avoid counterstrikes. After retiring to a relatively safe location, the weapon was reloaded. The gun buggies often operated in pairs during combat conditions. Other weapons modifications to the Land Rover included mounting 7.62mm M60 light machine guns or MILAN anti-tank missiles.

Series 2 and 2As also served as radio and communications vehicles, light cargo transports and medical evacuation ambulances in Vietnam. Others were modified as ceremonial vehicles with seating and handrails to accommodate dignitaries during parades or troop reviews. The 'gun buggies' served for approximately 30 years with the Australian Army, with the last of them withdrawn in the 1990s. ∎

Australian advisers train South Vietnamese soldiers on the M40 recoilless rifle. These were mounted on Land Rovers dubbed 'gun buggies'. *(Creative Commons Ward, Peter Anthony via Wikimedia Commons)*

This Australian Land Rover truck has been damaged by a mine along a dirt road in Vietnam. *(Creative Commons Walter Brewer via Wikimedia Commons)*

A Bell UH-1H Iroquois or 'Huey' at an air show in 2017. *(Creative Commons Airwolfhound via Wikimedia Commons)*

A quartet of US Marine Corps UH-1E helicopters in formation in 1970. *(US National Archives and Records Administration)*

BELL UH-1 IROQUOIS

The experimental XH-40 prototype produced by Bell Aircraft made its maiden flight on October 20, 1956, and within a few short years the helicopter was a legend, one of several weapons of war that became symbolic of American involvement in the Vietnam conflict.

Entering service in 1959 as the HU-1, its designation was changed to UH-1 when the USAF standardised its nomenclature in 1962. Officially, the utility helicopter was the UH-1 Iroquois, but to those familiar with it referred to it as the 'Huey'. One of the iconic helicopters of modern military history, more than 16,000 examples were manufactured in more than two dozen variants during a run that spanned four decades.

The first of these arrived in Vietnam in the late 1950s, and it was there that the nickname 'Huey' was coined. The UH-1 was everywhere, instantly recognisable by its wide body, tailored for the multiple roles envisioned for a true utility helicopter. Its versatility was readily apparent in wartime, serving first as an air ambulance to evacuate wounded from the battlefield. When such medical evacuation (medevac) missions,

known as 'dustoffs', were flown, the 'Huey' could accommodate six stretchers. More than two million combat casualties were extracted from the battlefield during the course of the war and such missions were among the most dangerous of the conflict. A wounded soldier in Vietnam usually reached a medical facility within an hour and more than 99% of those who were still alive 24 hours later survived the war.

The 'Huey' flew for the US Army, Navy and Air Force, as well as the South Vietnamese military and other allied forces in Vietnam, proving proficient in the search and rescue, airlift and

supply, electronic warfare and fire support roles. The navy deployed them equipped with machine guns in support of its riverine forces operating in the treacherous Mekong Delta and along other waterways in South Vietnam, while the air force deployed them with its 20th Special Operations Squadron to conduct covert reconnaissance missions and psychological warfare operations in Cambodia and Laos.

The 'Huey' achieved its greatest fame with the emergence of the doctrine of airmobile warfare in Vietnam. The helicopter was literally the modern-day iron horse that transported the US Army's air cavalry into action. The first such deployment took place in the valley of the River Ia Drang in November 1965, as elements of the Army's 7th Cavalry Regiment, 1st Division (Airmobile), engaging the North Vietnamese Army directly in a major battle for the first time in the war.

The helicopters regularly transported troops swiftly into a combat zone, landing sometimes in a hot LZ (landing zone) and taking enemy fire, then rapidly pulling the soldiers out when the time came. In doing so, airmobile tactics rendered the large-scale parachute operations of earlier wars virtually obsolete, ushering in a new era of air assault combat. The US Marine Corps also participated in airmobile operations in Vietnam.

The Hueys that made hazardous troop-carrying runs were dubbed 'slicks' and carried a crew of four, including the pilot, co-pilot, crew chief and door gunner. 'Slicks' were armed only with a pair of .30-calibre M-60 machine guns mounted at the doors on either side of the helicopter.

The exigencies of war gave rise to continuous modifications of 'Hueys' in the field. One of

The Bell XH-40 helicopter prototype prepares for take-off. *(US Army)*

Soldiers of the US 1st Battalion, 7th Cavalry, leap from their 'Huey' and take up firing positions at LZ 'X-Ray' during the Battle of the Ia Drang, November 1965. *(US Army)*

This typical suite of armament in a Huey gunship includes machine guns and rocket pods. *(Greg Goebel via Wikimedia Commons)*

the most significant was the introduction of substantial armament, reducing the vulnerability of the 'slicks' as they approached a hot LZ. As early as 1962, field modifications to some Hueys, such as external M-60 machine guns and rocket pods, allowed them to take on an escort role, providing suppressing fire while the 'slicks' delivered or extracted their human cargo. By 1963, a modified 'Huey' gunship was being produced in the UH-1C variant, capable of also carrying a 40mm grenade launcher mounted in the helicopter's chin. By 1967, the powerful, purpose-built AH-1 'Huey' Cobra Gunship was introduced.

The 'Huey' was easy to identify not only due to its distinctive profile, but also the hum of its main rotor blade powered by a turboshaft engine rather than the traditional piston engine that drove most helicopters of the era. The rugged, reliable turbine engine brought significantly enhanced performance over other contemporary types. Initially, the UH-1 was powered by the Lycoming YT53-L-1 that produced 700hp. By 1966, the Lycoming T53-L-13 had been introduced, increasing capability to 1,400hp and a top speed of 127mph in the UH-1H variant. The UH-1H carried up to 14 combat-ready infantrymen with a service ceiling of 12,600ft and range of 318 miles.

The Huey remains in service today with the armed forces of more than 40 countries. However, it was in Vietnam that it wrote a stirring chapter in military history. During the war, more than 12,000 helicopters of various types were in service. Roughly 5,000 of these were lost to enemy fire or accidents. According to official records, between 1966 and 1971, one US Army helicopter was lost for every 7.9 sorties flown. 'Huey' pilots and aircrew logged a phenomenal 7.5 million flight hours during the Vietnam conflict, while 5,000 of the famed helicopters saw service. Roughly half of these were lost in combat. ■

A Huey lifts off after delivering US troops during the Battle of the Ia Drang, November 1965. *(US Army)*

AH-1 COBRA

Bell AH-1G Cobra in service with the 3rd Squadron, 4th Cavalry, in Vietnam. *(US Army)*

Agile and armed to the teeth, the Bell AH-1 Cobra was the first purpose-built helicopter gunship or attack helicopter to enter military service.

A derivative of the Bell UH-1, the Cobra came into being with the realisation that close ground support in Vietnam was critical for both basic and airmobile operations. The 'Huey' had been fitted with machine guns to provide some security and defence against the enemy when delivering troops to a hot LZ (landing zone) in airmobile operations, but it had not been intended for that purpose.

Grasping the concept of the gunship and researching the prospects for a frontline model, Bell Helicopter's engineers brought the same engine, the Lycoming T53-L-703 with 1,800hp, a rotor system and other components together again, this time in a narrow, slimmed-down fuselage with an armoured cockpit that afforded stepped tandem seating for a commander and gunner. The commander occupied the higher second seat, while the gunner was forward and lower with a better field of vision. Both occupants were usually certified pilots, providing a tactical advantage in combat. The narrower fuselage diminished the enemy's ability to acquire the Cobra as a target, while the AH-1 carried an impressive array of weapons. In practice, the Cobra gunship flew escort duties with the 'Huey' in airmobile operations, delivering suppressing fire while combat troops were offloaded, or else in co-operation with the Hughes OH-6A Cayuse scout helicopter in a hunter-killer combination seeking targets of opportunity or vectored onto enemy troop concentrations and supply lines.

Its array of armament was often devastating to targets in the open. The Cobra was fitted with a combination of two 7.62mm multibarrel miniguns, two M129 40mm grenade launchers (or one of each), 2.75mm rockets fired from pods attached to stubby wing hard points, an M18 minigun pod or the XM35 armament subsystem mounting the XM195 20mm cannon.

The Cobra prototype, Model 209, first flew on September 7, 1965, and the first AH-1G helicopters reached Vietnam in the summer of 1967. Six AH-1H variants were delivered to Bien Hoa Air Base, South Vietnam, in August of that year for combat testing. The first recorded 'kill' by a Cobra crew occurred on September 4, 1967, when one of the gunships sank an enemy sampan and killed four Viet Cong guerrillas. A month later, the first AH-1 unit, the 334th Assault Helicopter Company, was declared operational. During the Vietnam conflict, Cobras flew more than a million combat hours. Their numbers in action peaked at 1,081, and 300 were lost to enemy action or operational accidents.

The Cobra flew in large numbers with US and allied forces into the 1990s, until it was replaced largely by the AH-64 Apache. However, some examples remain in service with the US Marine Corps and other friendly militaries. ■

An AH-1G Cobra gunship on a mission over Vietnam in 1968. *(US Army Heritage and Education Center)*

This Cobra carries some of the heavy armament that brought ground support firepower to the war in Vietnam. *(US Army)*

OH-6 CAYUSE

The Hughes OH-6 Cayuse was a familiar sight in the skies over Vietnam. Introduced as a light observation helicopter (LOH), its nickname quickly became the 'Loach'.

Hughes' Model 369 was the pick of three competing submissions (the others came from Bell and Fairchild-Hiller) that responded to US Army Technical Specification 153 distributed in 1960. The Model 369 served as the basis for a replacement for the Army's older Bell H-13 Sioux helicopter. By May 1965, Hughes received a production contract for the OH-6, which had taken its first flight on February 27, 1963.

Only 2,000 of the original OH-6, OH-6A and other derivatives were produced, although variants such as the Hughes MD 500 civilian helicopter and the MH-6 Little Bird utilised by US Special Forces, along with its well-known AH-6 attack variant, did emerge. In addition to reconnaissance, the 'Loach' performed transport, medical evacuation and close air support in Vietnam.

The production model OH-6A was crewed by a pilot and observer and was capable of hauling internal cargo up to 1,000lb. The powerplant was the Allison T63-A-5A turboshaft engine with four rotor blades and up to 317hp with a maximum speed of 150mph and a range of 380 miles. An engine upgrade in the OH-6B to the Allison T63-A-720 increased output to 420hp. The teardrop configuration offered excellent visibility,

An OH-6A participating in the Royal International Air Tattoo, Gloucestershire, in 2019. *(Creative Commons Steve Lynes via Wikimedia Commons)*

while armament consisted of a single 7.62mm machine gun or M75 40mm grenade launcher.

The first OH-6As were deployed to Vietnam in December 1967 and the versatile helicopter participated in observation, escort and hunter-killer missions alongside its partner, the Bell AH-1 Cobra gunship. The 'Loach' would typically fly low to observe and possibly attract enemy fire, then the Cobra unleashed a response to destroy the source. At times, the 'Loach' dropped a smoke grenade to mark the location of a camouflaged enemy position for the Cobra.

The 'Loach' also participated in clandestine operations for the Central Intelligence Agency. One of these was conducted in 1972 when modified OH-6As used sophisticated listening devices to eavesdrop on high-level North Vietnamese communications.

Contract disputes with Hughes limited the production of the 'Loach' and opened the door for the introduction of the Bell OH-58 Kiowa, which deployed to Vietnam in August 1969. The two types served concurrently during the war and both became more susceptible to enemy fire as the Soviet Union supplied shoulder-fired surface-to-air missiles to the North Vietnamese and Viet Cong. Over time, US helicopter tactics were modified to mitigate the threat.

Loss records vary greatly but assert that between 658 and 964 'Loaches' were shot down or otherwise destroyed in Vietnam. A total of 45 OH-58s were lost in the war. ■

Soldiers of the US 25th Infantry Division load captured North Vietnamese documents aboard a 'Loach' in May 1970. *(National Archives and Records Administration)*

An OH-6A flies in company with a pair of AH-1 Cobra gunships on a hunter-killer mission, Phuoc Vinh, Vietnam, 1970. *(US Army)*

CH-47 CHINOOK

With a hauling capacity of 22,000lb, the CH-47 Chinook was capable of transporting supplies and equipment or 55 fully loaded combat troops into an operational area in Vietnam. Loading was accomplished through rear and side doors, and cargo could also be carried externally.

Developed by Vertol, which was later acquired by Boeing, the Chinook was designed in the mid-1950s as a rotary turbine engine replacement for the earlier piston-engined Sikorsky CH-37 Mojave. Design competitions were held in 1958 and the US Army chose the Vertol entry for testing and eventual production. The prototype made its first flight on September 21, 1961, and the twin rotor helicopter's first operational variant, the CH-47A, entered service with the US Army

US soldiers of the 1st Cavalry Division (Airmobile) rush from a CH-47 Chinook in Vietnam, February 1966. *(National Archives and Records Administration)*

the following year. Since then, numerous upgrades and improvements have been made.

Powered by a pair of Lycoming T55 turboshaft engines, the CH-47 was capable of a top speed of 200mph with a service ceiling of 20,000ft when introduced. Its crew of three included a pilot, co-pilot and loadmaster. It is still being manufactured today and in 2012 at least 1,200 had been completed.

The first CH-47 arrived in Vietnam on November 29, 1965, to serve as primary medium lift air transport. By early 1966, more than 160 had arrived in country as the 1st Cavalry Division (Airmobile) brought its organic complement, a full battalion of three companies, to Southeast Asia. Defensive armament was provided with the installation of a pair of 7.62mm M60 light machine guns at each forward door. At times, a heavier Browning M2 .50-calibre machine gun was mounted to fire from the rear cargo door.

Although initial difficulties were encountered when ground commanders sought to overload the spacious cargo compartment and the transmission system of the CH-47A was found inadequate to support the two turbine engines when both were at full power, the CH-47B and CH-47C arrived in Vietnam, bringing greater horsepower with them. The climate of Vietnam did affect maximum lift capability, reducing it by about 20% in the coastal and lowland areas and 30% over higher altitude mountainous terrain.

At the height of the Vietnam war, 21 Chinook companies were operating in country and the type delivered outstanding support to airmobile warfare. It was capable of delivering troops, artillery pieces and other equipment into mountainous locations that might otherwise have been virtually inaccessible. While complementing the lighter UH-1 utility helicopter, the CH-47 became primarily a transporter of heavier weapons, ammunition and supplies.

An estimated 750 Chinooks entered service in Vietnam, 200 of which were lost to operational accidents or enemy fire. ■

A CH-47 Chinook hovers above a hillside in Vietnam in 1967 as troops and supplies are gathered below. *(US Army)*

A CH-47 Chinook carries an 105mm howitzer in a sling at Fire Support Base Challenge in Vietnam, April 1970. *(US Army)*

Crews flying the Sikorsky HH3E 'Jolly Green Giant' saved scores of American lives in Vietnam. *(Creative Commons Alan Wilson via Wikimedia Commons)*

HH3E JOLLY GREEN GIANT

For many American airmen downed in the jungles of Vietnam, the sight of a 'Jolly Green Giant' was one of hope, relief and rescue. An enduring image of the war in Southeast Asia is that of the intrepid crew of a Sikorsky HH3E hovering, amid enemy fire, to extract a pilot or aircrew member. The heroism of the 'Jolly Green Giant' crews is well known, and the helicopter they flew earned its place in modern military history.

The HH3E was a modified version of the Sikorsky CH-3 transport helicopter, specifically the CH-3E Sea King, and its role was combat air search and rescue. A total of 50 helicopters were modified with a rescue hoist, self-sealing fuel tanks, a large and powered rear ramp and defensive armament that included a pair of 7.62mm M60 machine guns. Capable of transporting up to 25 passengers or 15 stretchers and two medical personnel, the HH3E was driven by a pair of General Electric T58-GE-5 series turboshaft engines that generated 1,500hp, a top speed of 165mph and a range of 896 miles. Its crew of four included a pilot, co-pilot, flight mechanic and machine gunner.

Nicknamed the 'Jolly Green Giant', the HH3E arrived in Southeast Asia in 1967, and from its locations at Udorn Air Base in Thailand and the South Vietnamese coastal city of Da Nang, its range made the entire region accessible in the rescue role. It participated in the failed attempt to free American POWs from the Son Tay prison in 1970 because the North Vietnamese had relocated the prisoners prior to the raid.

During the course of the Vietnam conflict, 'Jolly Green Giant' aircrews rescued scores of downed airmen, earning 24 Air Force Crosses, 190 Silver Stars and a Medal of Honor in the process. The big HH3Es regularly absorbed direct enemy fire during rescue operations and it was not unusual for them to return from a mission with significant damage.

Perhaps the most famous of the type to serve in Vietnam was 'Jolly Green 22', now on display at the National Museum of the US Air Force in Dayton, Ohio. This served 32 months in country and survived a harrowing mission on March 14, 1968.

An HH3E 'Jolly Green Giant' in flight during exercises. *(US Department of Defense)*

Special Forces in the Son Tay Raid are shown aboard a 'Jolly Green Giant'. *(US Government)*

A US Marine Corps F-4 Phantom fighter bomber had been shot down, and though one of the airmen was recovered, the other remained missing when 'Jolly Green 22' was forced to withdraw due to enemy fire. The second airman was killed and the North Vietnamese attempted an ambush when 'Jolly Green 22' made a second run-in, the crew unaware that the missing Marine had died. The HH3E managed to escape the intense fire, returning to base with 68 bullet holes, its rotor blades riddled and a windshield shattered. At the end of its combat service, crewmen aboard 'Jolly Green 22' were credited with saving 27 downed airmen while earning 14 Silver Stars and an Air Force Cross. ■

T-54/55

The T-54/55 tank 843 that smashed through the gate of South Vietnam's Presidential Palace in Saigon on April 30, 1975, is shown on display in a museum. *(Creative Commons Z3144228 via Wikimedia)*

The Russian T-34 had become a legend during World War Two and Soviet tank designers hoped its successor, the T-44, would prove equally iconic. But the T-44 was perhaps a victim of the incredible velocity of improvements taking place in tank design in the waning months of the Great Patriotic War and into the Cold War.

The T-44 was produced only in small numbers, with about 2,000 completed by late 1945. In the middle of production, it was decided to adapt the chassis for the large D-10T 100mm rifled gun. The challenge involved the expansion of the turret ring, which in turn meant lengthening the T-44's hull. In combination with numerous other evolving aspects, these changes brought about the adoption of a new type altogether.

Designated the T-54, the new type went into production at facilities in Nizhny Tagil in 1947 and, a year later, at Kharkiv. At the same time, the classifications of light, medium and heavy tanks merged into the new ideal: the main battle tank. In that regard, the T-54 might well be considered the last Soviet medium tank. However, with nearly 1,500 alterations having been made to the earliest production T-54, engineer Leonid Kartsez of the OKB-520 Design Bureau at the Stalin Ural Tank Factory No. 183 advocated combining the ongoing improvements in the T-54 into the Object 155. In the spring of 1958, the new T-55 entered service with the Red Army.

Although the T-55 lacked an anti-aircraft machine gun, as had been mounted with the T-54, it did provide an improved powerplant, along with protection against nuclear, biological and chemical (NBC) weapons. Many T-54s were re-engineered as the T-55 over several years, with analysts often referring to the amalgamation – the blurred line between the two types – as the generic T-54/55.

From the mid-1940s into the 1980s, the T-54/55 was produced in greater numbers than any other tank in history. Some estimates of production numbers exceed 100,000, and many alterations and upgrades have occurred, resulting in numerous variations to the original platform. The tank has been in service with more than 50 countries, deployed in numerous conflicts across the globe and remains active with many armies to this day.

The appearance of the T-54/55 with its powerful main weapon also spurred the Soviet Union's Cold War adversaries to respond. The United States developed the M60 series of main battle tanks, while Great Britain introduced the superb 105mm Royal Ordnance L7 rifled gun to replace the QF 20-pounder weapon arming its Centurions.

The T-54/55 was manned by a crew of four, a driver in the hull and a commander, gunner and loader packed inside the cramped turret on the same side. The loader was required to manage several functions to service the main gun, which slowed down its rate of fire. However, it is worth noting that crew comfort was always a secondary consideration in Soviet tank design. The tank weighed nearly 40 tons, stood nearly 8ft tall and was 29½ft long. Its standard powerplant was the 520hp, V-12 Type V-54 diesel engine, generating a top road speed of 30mph and a range of 300 miles. Armour protection varied from nearly seven inches on the turret front to four inches forward on the hull and just over an inch on the roof of

T-54/55 Tank 843 in an outdoor display at the Independence Palace, Ho Chi Minh City. *(Creative Commons 源義信 via Wikimedia Commons)*

The original T-54 tank was manufactured in 1946. *(Creative Commons Nucl0id via Wikimedia Commons)*

T-54/55s and infantrymen advance along a dirt road in Vietnam. *(Creative Commons Hoangprs5 via Wikimedia Commons)*

Vietnamese children in Kontum climb aboard a destroyed T-54/55 knocked out during the Easter Offensive of 1972. *(Lấy từ ảnh của A. Abbas)*

the hull. Secondary armament varied over the years, but regularly included a coaxially mounted 7.62mm machine gun and a 12.7mm machine gun at the turret hatch for anti-aircraft defence.

The T-54/55 was delivered to North Vietnam by the late 1960s and saw action against US-made armour for the first time during Operation Lam Son 719, a South Vietnamese offensive in February 1971. The Army of the Republic of Vietnam (ARVN) 1st Armoured Brigade sent 17 M41 Walker Bulldog light tanks into action and reported destroying six T-54s and 16 amphibious PT-76 light tanks. However, in the larger combat of Lam Son 719, it is believed that five M41s and 25 M113 Armored Personnel Carriers were lost to North Vietnamese forces.

During the communist Easter Offensive of 1972, the ARVN 1st Squadron, 20th Tank Regiment, deployed 57 M48 Patton tanks in ambush against advancing North Vietnamese armour, striking near the town of Dong Ha on April 2 and destroying a pair of T-54s and nine PT-76s. A week later, the entire 20th Regiment engaged T-54s and accompanying infantry. The ARVN tankers claimed to have destroyed 16 T-54s, but records place the loss at only six. No ARVN tanks were lost and a Chinese-made Type 59, a virtual clone of the T-54, was captured.

In the same month, 18 T-54s and accompanying infantry attacked the ARVN 22nd Infantry Division base camp at Tan Canh, routing the defenders and reportedly destroying 18 M41s and 31 M113s. A single T-54, No. 377, was reported to have knocked out seven M41s before it was destroyed by a man portable M72 LAW anti-tank missile. Another 17 M41s were captured. North Vietnamese losses were only two T-54s and a single PT-76.

One of the lasting images of the Vietnam war is that of a Viet Cong T-54/55 tank smashing through the gate of the Presidential Palace in Saigon, the South Vietnamese capital, on April 30, 1975, its flag whipping in the breeze. The action symbolised the fall of the South Vietnamese government and the ultimate communist victory in the long war in Southeast Asia. ■

A North Vietnamese T-54/55 tank raises a cloud of dust during exercises. *(Creative Commons Hoangprs5 via Wikimedia Commons)*

A T-34/85 on display in a Russian museum. *(Creative Commons Участник:Shura007 via Wikimedia Commons)*

T-34/85

Produced in greater numbers than any other tank during World War Two, the Soviet T-34 was a war winner. Its 60° sloped armour, speed and firepower were recognized as significant attributes and, a generation later, the type was still in service with the armed forces of the Soviet client state of North Vietnam.

The basic T-34 design was completed during a three-year period from 1937 to 1940 and its suspension was the brainchild of American engineer J Walter Christie. The T-34 proved ideally suited for the Soviet concept of deep battle. Its effectiveness as a penetration weapon was demonstrated with its introduction on the Eastern Front and, in addition to its battlefield capability, its reasonable cost and ease of assembly were critical to the Soviet war effort.

More than 84,000 T-34s were built in the Soviet Union between 1940 and 1946, with production continuing in Czechoslovakia and Poland into the 1950s. With a crew of four, the initial T-34 mounted a 76.2mm main gun, along with secondary armament of two 7.62mm DT machine guns for protection against infantry and low-flying aircraft. The tank weighed 29.2 tons and its armour protection varied from 15mm on the bottom of the hull to 60mm for areas of the turret and 47mm for the frontal hull. The original engine was the 500hp Model V-2-34 V-12 diesel, delivering a top speed of 33mph. Upgrades for enhanced performance were introduced over the years.

By 1944, the Soviets were producing the T-34/85, an improvement on the original design that featured a more powerful 85mm

This T-34/85 is now a monument on public display in Vietnam. *(Creative Commons Langlebigkeit Manie via Wikimedia Commons)*

A T-34/85 in Red Square, Moscow, during the 2018 Victory Day parade. *(Creative Commons Russian Presidential Press and Information via Wikimedia Commons)*

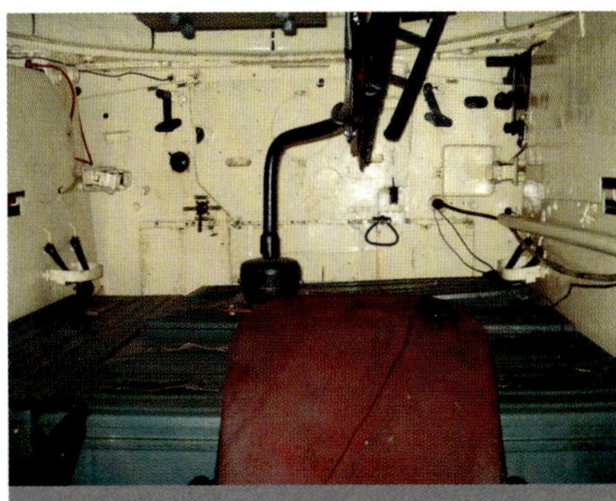

This interior view of the T-34/85 tank reveals little regard for creature comforts. *(Creative Commons Balcer-commonswiki via Wikimedia Commons)*

T-34/85 tanks are shown with German types from World War Two during a re-enactment in 2016. *(Creative Commons Vitaly V. Kuzmin via Wikimedia Commons)*

Zis-S-53 main gun, along with increased armour protection varying from 20mm to 90mm. The T-34/85's weight increased to 35 tons with a maximum range of 193 miles cross-country and 301 miles on improved roads. By the end of World War Two, more than 22,000 of the improved tank had been built.

By 1959, the People's Army of North Vietnam was establishing an armoured component and its first tanks were T-34/85s. Most of these had been modernised before delivery, including the same 'starfish' road wheels as the later T-54/55 and other modifications. Some of the tanks were outfitted in North Vietnam with a DShK 12.7mm external machine gun, an effective anti-aircraft weapon. The T-34/85M or Model 1969 is most associated with the North Vietnamese forces and incorporated improved R-123 radio communications apparatus and greater fuel capacity, along with drivetrain improvements and the addition of night-vision equipment.

The T-34/85 was primarily used in an infantry support role or as mobile artillery. Its offensive capability was limited by the primitive North Vietnamese tactics and the intentional avoidance of direct tank vs tank engagements. The tanks were sometimes committed without screening infantry or in relatively few numbers.

The first notable employment of communist armour was in response to Operation Lam Son 719 in early 1971. South Vietnamese forces launched an offensive intended to sever the Ho Chi Minh Trail, the route of troop infiltration and resupply from the north via Laos and Cambodia. While US forces provided air and artillery support, the North Vietnamese organised a response code named the Route 9 Operation. The 297th Tank Battalion with 33 T-54/55 tanks, the 198th Tank Battalion with 22 PT-76 light tanks and the 397th Tank Battalion with 33 T-34/85s were deployed.

The communist tanks confronted a South Vietnamese armoured brigade of 66 M41 Walker Bulldog light tanks and took serious losses. While the PT-76s and T-54/55s bore the brunt of the direct engagement with a US estimate of six T-54/55s and 17 PT-76s destroyed, the T-34/85s were held in reserve. Although their action was limited, the World War Two-vintage tanks were known for their mechanical reliability in the field and their performance in the jungles and difficult terrain.

In 1972, The Soviet Union sent approximately 400 tanks to North Vietnam and a battalion of up to 48 T-34/85s was included. During the subsequent Easter Offensive, the communist forces crossed the demilitarised zone in strength. Two tank regiments were committed to the offensive, and at least 60 of these were T-34/85s. The older tanks were initially impressive in their deployment. However, the appearance of the modern M48 Patton tanks of the South Vietnamese came as a rude surprise, while heavy bombing helped bring the communist offensive to a halt.

The most devastating loss of T-34/85s occurred during a refuelling stop, when as many as 30 were caught in the open and wiped out during a heavy bombing strike delivered by the B-52 Stratofortresses of the US Air Force. A total of 40 T-34/85 tanks were lost during the Easter Offensive and the remaining available examples were withdrawn to an armoured reserve after covering the withdrawal of the North Vietnamese and Viet Cong forces from some areas. There are no confirmed records of a T-34/85 destroying an opposing armoured vehicle in tank vs tank combat in Vietnam.

In addition to the fighting that occurred in South Vietnam, the T-34/85 was also involved in operations in northern Laos in support of the communist Pathet Lao. The T-34/85 was utilised aggressively in Laos in the 1970s as the anti-tank capabilities of the government troops that opposed them were quite limited. During the fighting in the Laotian Xieng Khouang Province, the T-34/85 was quite effective in infantry support. Extended deployments there were facilitated by its rugged construction and ease of maintenance. ■

This T-34/85 sits at the entrance to a museum in the Vietnamese city of Da Nang. *(Creative Commons Mztourist via Wikimedia Commons)*

PT-76

In 1964, the North Vietnamese government requested 500 PT-76 light amphibious tanks from its Soviet benefactors and these were delivered between 1965 and 1973. During the period, the armoured forces of the communist military increased substantially from a lone tank battalion to three regiments by 1971.

Although many of the PT-76s received from the Soviets had previously been used by the Red Army, they were quite serviceable and were utilised by the communists in offensive operations on several occasions. The amphibious light tank was effective against unsupported troop concentrations and light fortifications, but it proved quite vulnerable to the heavy-calibre guns of US M48 Patton tanks and American-made anti-tank missiles.

The PT-76, which the Vietnamese called 'Xe thiet giap' or 'ironclad', was a post-war example of the Soviet tradition of equipping its armoured units with light amphibious tanks. In 1949, engineer N Shashmurin presented a blueprint labelled 'Object 740' in collaboration with engineer Josef Kotin at the Kirov Tank Plant, and the prototype was constructed at the Chelyabinsk Tank Plant VNII-100 Institute (ChTz) near Leningrad.

Generally described as a lengthened version of the World War Two-era T-40 tank, the PT-76 was approved for mass production on August 6, 1951. In standard form, the driver sat forward in the centre of the hull, with the commander and loader positioned inside the low, cone-shaped turret. The commander was also tasked as the gunner and radio operator, taxing his capabilities to exert control during combat situations. The hull was constructed of welded, cold rolled steel and varied in thickness from .3in on the roof to more than ¾in on the front glacis with an enhancing slope of 20°. The protection was effective only against small-arms fire, some flash burns and shell fragments.

The PT-76 weighed just over 16 tons, stood 7¾ft high and was 25ft long. Its primary armament was the 76.2mm D-56T rifled gun

PT-76 light amphibious tank on display at the Verkhnyaya Pyshma Tank Museum in Sverdlovsk Oblast, Russia. *(Creative Commons Владимир Саппинен via Wikimedia Commons)*

,while secondary armament consisted of a single 7.62mm machine gun. The powerplant was the 240hp, six-cylinder V-6B diesel engine generating a top road speed of 27mph and a range of 230 miles. For amphibious operations, bilge pumps were switched on and a pair of water jets added propulsion. Approximately 12,000 PT-76 tanks were built through 1969.

In Vietnam, the PT-76 proved somewhat limited in its amphibious capability due to its sheer size, but gave an overall solid performance regarding mobility. Its real disadvantage came where it counted most – its thin armour was incapable of

withstanding the heavy 90mm gun of the M48 Patton tank and an array of anti-tank weapons.

The PT-76 was involved in several firefights with US and South Vietnamese forces. In early February 1968, 13 PT-76s of the North Vietnamese 202nd Armoured Regiment formed the vanguard of the assault on the South Vietnamese/US Special Forces camp at Lang Vei. The base was overrun, but the tanks suffered at least four losses to the 106mm recoilless rifle and M72 LAW man portable 66mm light anti-tank weapon.

The first reported action between the PT-76 and US-built armour occurred near the Ben Hai River near the demilitarised zone (DMZ) along the frontier of Laos in central Vietnam. The crew of a PT-76 was observed by an American reconnaissance aircraft while washing their vehicle. The information was relayed to elements of the US 3rd Tank Battalion, and an M48 rumbled forward as the aircraft

Destroyed during fighting in northern Laos decades ago, this PT-76 remains in a densely wooded area. *(Creative Commons PTD Phonsavan via Wikimedia Commons)*

US soldiers inspect the wreckage of one of two PT-76 light amphibious tanks destroyed during the battle of Ben Het in March 1968. *(US Army)*

A Soviet PT-76 rolls down a street in Budapest during unrest in Hungary in 1956. *(Creative Commons Nagy Gyula via Wikimedia Commons)*

assisted with location and fire adjustment. The Patton's third 90mm round struck the PT-76 and its crew promptly fled the area.

In March 1969, the battle of Ben Het brought the PT-76 and US Army tanks in direct confrontation, and it is remembered as the only tank vs tank battle of consequence during the entire American experience in Southeast Asia. On March 3, the Special Forces camp at Ben Het near the border of South Vietnam, Laos and Cambodia came under attack by communist small arms, mortars, recoilless rifles and armour. In the North Vietnamese advance, a PT-76 of the 16th Company, 4th Battalion, 202nd Armoured Regiment, struck a mine. The resulting explosion disabled the tank and exposed others nearby to American fire, which promptly disabled a BTR-50 tracked armoured personnel carrier.

In the ensuing melee, a PT-76 managed a hit that struck an M48, causing only light damage but killing two crewmen and wounding two US 5th Special Forces soldiers. A second crew was dispatched to the Patton, which returned to action moments later. One American soldier ran toward an M48 that was not in position to fire on the enemy and reoriented the crew to enter the engagement. Seconds later, the Patton fired a 90mm round that destroyed the targeted PT-76. The North Vietnamese attack faltered, and orders were issued to withdraw. The defenders suffered only one damaged M48, three killed and eight wounded. Although North Vietnamese casualties are unknown, 2 PT-76s and a BTR-50 were lost.

On May 9, 1972, the recently deployed wire-guided American BGM-71 TOW missile scored its first armour kill. After completing training in country, the 1st Combat Aerial TOW Team flew aboard Bell UH-1B helicopters mounting the TOW in three-tube launchers on a search-and-destroy mission against enemy armour. The Special Forces camp at Ben Het was again under attack and the TOW missiles quickly blasted three PT-76s, thwarting the communist assault. Two weeks later, the TOW took its toll again. This time an attack on the city of Kontum was repulsed with the missiles, destroying nine communists tanks, four of them PT-76s. Another PT-76 was damaged in the engagement. ■

These PT-76 light amphibious tanks were knocked out during fighting at Lang Vei, probably by an American 106mm recoilless rifle. *(US Air Force)*

The PT-76 was vulnerable to large-calibre guns and anti-tank missiles. *(Creative Commons Gonzo Gooner via Wikimedia Commons)*

TYPE 59

The Soviet Union and the People's Republic of China signed the Treaty of Friendship, Alliance, and Mutual Assistance in 1956. Along with the agreement came co-operation in military projects and arms production.

A significant aspect of the technology transfer that resulted from the treaty was the manufacturing of armoured fighting vehicles. With Soviet assistance, the Chinese enhanced vehicle production at their facility in the north of the country in 1954. The 617 Institute Inner Mongolia No 1 Machinery Plant near the city of Bautou was dedicated to the production of the Type 59 main battle tank. A direct copy of the early Soviet T-54A, the first Chinese-produced Type 59s were built with parts supplied by Russia.

The Chinese initially called the tank the WZ-120 and it was accepted into service with the People's Liberation Army (PLA) in 1959. Several hundred were later sent to the North Vietnamese Army and used during the protracted war with the South Vietnamese and their US benefactors. While tank vs tank combat was rare in Vietnam, the Type 59 was among the most active communist tanks throughout.

Production of the Type 59 continued through 1985 as upgrades were introduced, with 9,500 eventually built. The tank resembled its Soviet precursor, with a dome-shaped turret centrally located atop the hull and an engine compartment to the rear. The driver sat forward and to the left in the hull, while the commander, gunner and loader were in the turret, commander to the left, gunner forward and below and the loader to the right. The turret mounted the Type 59 rifled 100mm cannon, with 34 rounds typically carried aboard. Secondary armament included the Type 54 12.7mm anti-aircraft machine gun mounted by the gunner's turret hatch and the Type 59T 7.62mm machine gun mounted in the hull and operated by the driver. A second Type 59T was mounted coaxially with the main gun.

The early Type 59 lacked the gun stabilisation equipment of the T-54, but the Chinese made improvements through acquired Soviet or Western technology. For example, when a Soviet T-62 tank was captured during the brief Sino-Soviet border clash in 1969, upgrades were made that led to the classification of a new Chinese tank, the Type 69. Later modifications led to the Type 79, the final first-generation Chinese main battle tank. The types were used by the PLA and exported to numerous countries, with many Type 59 derivatives forming the backbone of the PLA armoured force roughly until the early 2000s.

The early powerplant was the 520hp V-12 M12150L diesel engine, delivering a top speed of 31mph and a range of 373 miles. Armour protection ranged from 20-203mm and the tank weighed 40 tons. It stood just over 8½ft high and was nearly 20ft long. ∎

Type 59 tank on display at the Reunification Palace in Ho Chi Minh City, Vietnam. *(Creative Commons Vyacheslav Argenberg via Wikimedia Commons)*

South Vietnamese soldiers atop a captured Type 59 tank south of Dong Ha, Vietnam. *(US Army)*

An immobilised Type 59, probably hit by a TOW anti-tank missile, on a street in the South Vietnamese town of An Loc in 1972. *(US Air Force)*

TYPE 62

The Type 59 main battle tank was powerful but heavy and not well suited for the mountainous terrain, river crossings and rice paddies of southern China. Therefore, the People's Liberation Army (PLA) requested the development of a light tank that would offer better mobility and the result was the Type 62.

Development of the light tank was undertaken at Factory 674, the Harbin First Machinery Building Group, in 1958. The first prototype was ready for testing by 1960 and, three years later, production was begun for the PLA. Nearly 1,400 were built by the time production ended in 1989.

Originally known as the WZ-131, the original Type 62 featured a cast steel turret with smaller steel hull and amour protection ranging from 12.5mm on the underside and top to 50mm on the turret. The standard interior layout included an engine compartment to the rear with the driver forward in the hull and the commander, loader and gunner in the turret and central combat space.

The Type 62 mounted the 85mm Type 62-85TC rifled main gun, with 47 rounds carried aboard. Secondary armament consisted of coaxial and bow mounted 7.62mm Type 59T machine guns.

The first major upgrade, the Type 62-I, included laser range-finding equipment and a 12.7mm anti-aircraft machine gun with shield mount. The late production Type 62G mounted a 105mm main gun with stabilisation and modern fire control features, but these improvements emerged only after the Sino-Vietnamese War of 1979.

The early Type 62 was initially sent to areas of southern China, then transferred to

Chinese Type 62 light tank at the Beijing Military Museum. *(Max Smith Public Domain)*

North Vietnamese Army units in substantial numbers. About 200 were involved in communist offensive action in the early 1970s, but roughly half of these were destroyed or damaged in combat. Heavy losses occurred due to US and South Vietnamese artillery, attack helicopters and fixed wing aircraft, as well as the TOW anti-tank missile. Despite resembling a smaller scale Type 59, the Type 62's armour protection was found to be inadequate in action.

Nevertheless, the tank was mobile in difficult country, powered by the 430hp V12 12150L-3 diesel engine. Its top speed was 37mph on improved roads and a strong 22mphr cross country, with a range of 311 miles. The Type 62 stood just over 7½ft high and was 9½ft wide and weighed just over 23 tons.

After the Sino-Vietnamese War, the Type 62 was relegated to reconnaissance and fire support. It was withdrawn from service by 2013, but remains in operation with the forces of at least 10 nations, mostly in Asia and Africa. ■

This Type 62 light tank on display in Vientiane, Laos, was in action from 1971-1973. *(Creative Commons Chaoborus via Wikimedia Commons)*

A Chinese Type 62 at the Military Museum of the People's Revolution in Beijing. *(Creative Commons Tyg728 via Wikimedia Commons)*

TYPE 63

Type 63 tank on display in the Beijing Military Museum. *(Max Smith Public Domain)*

A Type 63 light amphibious tank destroyed in combat in Vietnam. *(US Government)*

Although the Chinese Type 63 amphibious light tank bears a striking resemblance to the Soviet PT-76, it was not built as a complete copy. After obtaining several examples of the PT-76 in the mid-1950s, the Chinese decided to construct their own version with similar capabilities by the autumn of 1958.

The 201 Institute and 615 Factory worked on an early prototype, the WZ-211 or Type 60, but testing proved a disappointment and the People's Liberation Army (PLA) instructed the Military Engineering Institute and the No. 60 Research Institute of Fifth Ministry of Machine Building to come up with a better test vehicle. Completed in 1962, this second prototype was sent to Norinco (China North Industries Group Corporation) Factory 615 and the Shaanxi Weiyang Diesel Engine Plant for further evaluation. The PLA approved the design, which entered production in the spring of 1963 and was officially designated Type 63.

The Type 63 production run included more than 1,550 vehicles in several variants, and the tank is believed to have been involved in combat for the first time during the North Vietnamese and Viet Cong Easter Offensive of 1972. The tank was originally powered by a 240hp, six-cylinder diesel engine, but this had a tendency to overheat and few examples of the early Type 63 were completed before a new variant, the Type 63-I, went into production with the improved 402hp, 12-cylinder 12150-L2 diesel engine, generating a top speed of nearly 40mph on improved roads, more than 18mph cross country and 7½mph in water. The trade-off for the better engine was a slight increase in weight from just over 20 tons to nearly 22 tons.

Although it resembled the PT-76, the Type 63 series made a structural change by mounting the turret in the centre of the boat-like hull rather than forward, while the Chinese-built hull was taller at 10¼ft, longer at nearly 28ft, and even deeper than the Soviet type. The Type 63 carried a four-man crew and the driver's position was located in the hull to the left rather than in the centre. The elliptical Type 60 turret was held over from the first prototype and mounted the Type 62-85TC 85mm rifled gun, identical to that of the Type 62, with 47 rounds of ammunition. Secondary armament included a coaxial 7.62mm machine gun, a 12.7mm anti-aircraft machine gun and a second 7.62mm machine gun depending on variant.

The Type 63 was equipped with a snorkel and exhibited good characteristics in difficult terrain and water. However, its thin armour protection, ranging from 10mm to 14mm, was only adequate against small-arms fire and shell fragments. An upgraded Type 63 remains in service today with the PLA and the armed forces of several other countries. ■

The boat-like hull of the Type 63 light amphibious tank. *(Creative Commons Tyg728 via Wikimedia Commons)*

The SU-76 was built in greater numbers during World War Two than any other armoured vehicle except the T-34 medium tank. *(Public Domain LostArtilleryMan via Wikimedia Commons)*

SU-76

With the exception of the T-34 medium tank, the SU-76 light self-propelled tank destroyer or assault gun was produced in greater numbers by the Soviet Union than any other armoured vehicle of World War Two. Post-war, the SU-76 was widely used by Soviet client states, with many examples going to the North Vietnamese Army.

Combat experience during the Great Patriotic War indicated to the Soviet military establishment the need for a self-propelled assault gun or tank destroyer to support Red Army infantry units in combat against the Nazis on the Eastern Front, with Russian units in action having witnessed the firepower and effectiveness of German self-propelled guns firsthand. In June 1942, the Soviet State Defence Committee (GKO) issued requirements for the design of mobile weapons mounting both the 76.2mm ZIS-3 field gun and the M3 122mm howitzer.

Earlier experiments had been conducted utilising the chassis of the obsolete T-26 light tank but, by the autumn of 1941, SA Ginzburg, chief designer of the People's Commissariat of the Tank Industry, had chosen to lengthen the chassis of the T-70 light tank with the addition of a road wheel on either side. A fully enclosed casemate with steel roof was placed at the rear of the hull, with the driver sat forward and the commander, gunner and loader in the casemate. The 76.2mm main gun was fixed in position to

SU-76 displayed in a military museum in Romania. *(Creative Commons Lupishor via Wikimedia Commons)*

fire from the casemate, with a maximum rate of up to 20 rounds per minute with an experienced crew. Its muzzle velocity generated enough penetrating power to destroy German light tanks and even the medium PzKpfw. V Panther with a well-placed shot. However, its best hope of disabling the heavy Tiger was to fire at the exposed tracks or the lighter armoured rear.

The new SU-76 entered service in December 1942 and four self-propelled artillery regiments were equipped with it by the spring of 1943. A total of 560 were built, but mechanical issues arose within days of deployment. The cross-country capability and firepower

had been welcomed by the Red Army, but these positive attributes were negated by persistent problems with the transmission. Many of the vehicles failed in the field and production was suspended in March 1943.

A formal inquiry into the failure of the SU-76's initial deployment was convened in the winter of 1943. When it was determined that the faulty transmission arrangement was the cause, Ginzburg was blamed for the defect. He was ousted and assigned as head of tank repair services for the 32nd Tank Brigade, 29th Tank Corps, but was killed in action. Ginzburg had

Painted in a camouflage scheme, this SU-76M is on display at the Tank Museum, Bovington, UK. *(Creative Commons LordHarris via Wikimedia Commons)*

An SU-76M captured during the Korean War, 1950. *(US Marine Corps)*

SU-76M in Budapest, Hungary, during the 1956 uprising. *(Creative Commons ETH-Bibliothek Zürich, Bildarchiv / Fotograf: Metzger, Jack / Com_M05-0448-0023 / CC BY-SA 4.0 via Wikimedia Commons)*

previously been recognised as being among the foremost tank designers in the Soviet Union and it has been said that when Premier Josef Stalin received news that he had been sent to the front an effort to recall the gifted engineer failed when the communication was not delivered in time.

Meanwhile, the Gorky Automobile Plant (GAZ) and Plant No. 38 competed to produce an improved version of the SU-76. The SU-15 prototype was tested in the summer of 1943, and GAZ engineers NA Astrov and AA Lipgart sorted the transmission problem by repositioning the twin 70hp, six-cylinder GAZ-203 petrol engines. They also discarded the casemate's steel roof in favour of an open top and the option of a canvas cover. With the removal of the roof, the ingress and egress of the crew was improved, and the vehicle became substantially lighter. The new configuration was adopted officially as the SU-76M and production resumed in the autumn of 1943 with GAZ, Plant No. 38, and Plant No. 40 turning out vehicles. When production ended in October 1945, nearly 14,000 SU-76Ms had been completed. More than 9,000

of the total output were built by GAZ, which became the primary supplier from January 1944 through to the end of World War Two.

Remaining in service with the Red Army into the 1950s, the SU-76M was exported to several nations and saw combat with North Korean forces from 1950-1953. The People's Republic of China, East Germany, Czechoslovakia, Romania and Poland also operated the SU-76, along with North Vietnam.

In addition to the main 76.2mm gun, the SU-76M mounted a 7.62mm machine gun. The vehicle weighed more than 23,000lb, stood nearly 7ft high and was over 16ft long. Its engines provided a top speed of 45mph. While its amour ranged from 10mm to 35mm

and offered only minimal protection, the open top made the vehicle even more susceptible to small-arms fire and shoulder-fired anti-tank weapons. The SU-76M required close infantry support when engaged in the field, and it was particularly vulnerable to hand grenades and other weapons in street-to-street urban fighting. Nevertheless, the manoeuvrability and firepower of the SU-76M were deemed adequate trade-offs for the diminished protection of the crew.

The final assessment of the SU-76M's combat performance reveals a simply constructed, rugged, and versatile self-propelled weapon that proved popular among the infantry units it fought beside. ■

SU-76M in the collection of the Bundeswehrmuseum in Dresden, Germany. Note the high-profile casemate. *(Creative Commons Jan Rehschuh via Wikimedia Commons)*

SU-100

On response to the firepower of Nazi armour, the Soviet Union developed several self-propelled tank destroyers during World War Two. These became progressively more powerful as the war progressed, with upgunning being the order of the day.

Following the success of the SU-76, the S-85 was developed with a more powerful 85mm main gun. However, the concurrent improvement programme that replaced the 76.2mm gun on the highly successful T-34 medium tank and brought about the T-34/85 meant the useful life of the SU-85 was short. The T-34/85 mounted the same weapon in a 360° traversing turret, while the SU-85 was a stationary mount. Therefore, the tank destroyer model was rendered unnecessary.

With the SU-85 going by the wayside, the obvious conclusion reached was that an even larger gun should be mounted in a tank destroyer. Enter the SU-100, named in reference to its 100mm high-velocity, long-barrelled D10-S gun. The SU-100 was quite similar in configuration to the SU-85 and retained some of its characteristics, including a 55° sloping casemate that gave the vehicle greater survivability, enhancing the effectiveness of its 2.95in armour on the frontal glacis to withstand high-calibre German shells up to 125mm. The SU-100 also carried over the addition of the SU-85 commander's cupola, along with a wider workspace that was accommodated in a sponson on the right-hand side of the hull.

LI Gorlitsky, chief designer of medium self-propelled guns for the Red Army, established

The forward casemate and length of the SU-100's big gun are visible in this image. *(Creative Commons Frano Atirador via Wikimedia Commons)*

Object 138 in early 1944. Work on the SU-100 prototype began in earnest even as the new 100mm gun was undergoing evaluation. Among multiple prospects, the D10-S, the long-barrelled version of the D-5 gun and a product of Constructors Bureau of Artillery Factory No. 9, was chosen for production. Nearly 5,000 SU-100s were built at the Ural Heavy Machinery Factory in Yekaterinburg. The SU-100 weighed 30½ tons, and its 500hp, 12-cylinder Model V-2-34M diesel engine delivered a top road speed of 30mph. Its crew of four included a commander, driver, gunner and loader.

The SU-100 made its combat debut in October 1944 and performed well during the Red Army offensive that resulted in the capture of the German capital of Berlin in 1945. However, there was no machine gun mounted to provide secondary armament, and the SU-100 required cover against enemy air attack or infantry assault, particularly in close quarters such as city streets.

At least 100 SU-100s are known to have been delivered to the North Vietnamese Army and its use as an assault gun was likely more prevalent than as a tank destroyer due to the relatively few armoured clashes documented during the conflict. The SU-100 is believed to still be in service with numerous nations and is probably in reserve with the Vietnamese Army today. ■

SU-100 self-propelled anti-tank gun on display at the Museum of the Great Patriotic War in Kiev, Ukraine. *(Creative Commons ChrisO via Wikimedia Commons)*

World War Two-era SU-100 at the Military Historical Museum of Artillery, Engineering Troops and Signal Corps, St Petersburg, Russia. *(Creative Commons Alf van Beem via Wikimedia Commons)*

The Soviet-built SU-122 self-propelled howitzer entered service with the Red Army during the waning months of World War Two. *(Republic of Poland)*

SU-122

Although some conjecture surrounds whether the Soviet-built SU-122, a self-propelled howitzer intended for infantry support and indirect fire, was a participant in Vietnam, it has been included here for two reasons. The SU-122 provided a link in the chain of Soviet armoured vehicle evolution and it is indicative of the firepower available in support of the communist North Vietnamese Army and Viet Cong insurgency.

The SU-122 was developed from the spring of 1942 through to the end of that year in response to the battlefield success achieved by German forces with their Sturmgeschutz III self-propelled assault gun and its 75mm main weapon. The Uralsky Machine Building Factory (UZTM) began work on a combination of a 76.2mm ZiS-3 field gun and the chassis of a T-34 medium tank, realising that the firepower was the same as the T-34 but that the absence of a turret would make the assault gun cheaper and faster to produce. This project was named U-34 and was led by design bureau engineers GF Ksjunin and NW Kurin. At the same time, a prototype mounting the 122mm M-30 howitzer from the design bureau of FF Petrov atop the chassis of captured Sturmgeschutz vehicles was built, but only 20 examples, dubbed SG-122, were completed.

While neither the U-34 nor the SG-122 was destined to enter production, UZTM designers continued to work with the two prototypes, pairing the improved M-30S 122mm howitzer with the T-34 chassis. By November 1942, the resulting U-35 test vehicle was approved with minimal modifications. The same chassis and turretless configuration were utilised, and when testing was completed in December, the U-35 went into production despite some known shortcomings regrading the mechanics of the howitzer and ventilation of the crew space.

Renamed the SU-35, then the SU-122, the vehicle became the first purpose-built Red Army assault gun of the war. It weighed just over 34 tons. Its frontal armour was 1.77in thick and sloped for enhanced protection of the five-man crew, including a commander, driver, gunner and two loaders. The 493hp, V-12 Klimov Model V-2 diesel engine produced a top road speed of 34mph, with a range of 190 miles with supplementary fuel tanks. There was no secondary armament, so the SU-122 was dependent on the close proximity of the infantry it was supporting in the field for security.

Although the SU-122 was intended for direct infantry assault and indirect fire support, its big howitzer could take on the 75mm and 88mm guns of the German PzKpfw. V Panther and PzKpfw VI Tiger if necessary and possibly prevail, meaning it gained a degree of popularity with the frontline units of the Red Army. However, heavier self-propelled guns were in the design phase and the production run of the SU-122 ended before the spring of 1945, probably with fewer than 1,200 built (sources vary as to the termination date and the number of vehicles completed). ■

SU-122 self-propelled howitzer at the Kubink Tank Museum near Moscow. *(Creative Commons Alan Wilson via Wikimedia Commons)*

The short-barrelled 122mm howitzer of the SU-122 was intended to defeat enemy strongpoints and provide indirect fire in infantry support. *(Creative Commons Saiga20K via Wikimedia Commons)*

ZSU-57-2

A crew of six operated the vehicle, comprising a commander, driver, gunner, sight adjuster and two loaders, and the twin 57mm autocannons fired up to 240 rounds per minute with a maximum vertical range of nearly 29,000ft, bringing even high-altitude aircraft into range.

By the time the SU-57-2 production run ended in 1960, more than 2,000 had been built in the Soviet Union. At least 500 examples of the ZSU-57-2 remained with the communist forces after the Vietnam war ended in 1975, with at least 200 believed to still be in service today. ■

The ZSU-57-2 was the first self-propelled anti-aircraft weapon to enter full production in the Soviet Union. *(Creative Commons VargaA via Wikimedia Commons)*

From the beginning of American involvement in Vietnam, the US Army, Navy, Air Force and Marine Corps enjoyed nominal air superiority. However, as the conflict progressed, North Vietnamese and Viet Cong air defences grew more robust. With aircraft becoming vulnerable during varied missions it inevitably led to the losses of many fixed and rotor-driven aircraft.

The ZSU-57-2, the first self-propelled antiaircraft gun to enter sustained production in the Soviet Union, was one of the earliest means of air defence provided to the communist forces during the war. In February 1946, Design Bureau No. 174 in Omsk had partnered with Research Institute No. 58 at Kaliningrad near Moscow to equip the chassis of the T-34 medium tank with 37mm anti-aircraft guns, but the design had been shelved in favour of the T-54 medium tank. Subsequently, engineer VG Grabin led the development of the twin 57mm S-68 anti-aircraft autocannon, an adaptation for the T-54 chassis based on the existing S-60 weapon. After testing, the project was labelled Object 500 and the first prototype was completed in June 1950. Improvements were made through six additional prototypes, but a shortage of the S-68A gun halted progress for months. Finally, testing concluded in December 1954 and the newly named ZSU-57-2 entered service with the Red Army in February 1955.

The ZSU-57-2 was sent to Vietnam in large numbers and reportedly was observed in action for the first time during the Easter Offensive of 1972. The mobile system was intended to provide cover for North Vietnamese ground troops against US and South Vietnamese air attack. It is also known to have operated in defence of the North Vietnamese 201st and 202nd Tank Regiments during the Easter Offensive, one of the few times organised communist armoured units were deployed in strength. Like US-made mobile anti-aircraft systems, the ZSU-57-2 was also used in ground support, with its 57mm twin guns defeating enemy strongpoints.

With an open, box-like turret, the ZSU-57-2 was driven by the 520hp, V-12 V-54 diesel engine, producing a top speed of 31mph and range of 261 miles on the road. It weighed nearly 31 tons and stood almost 9ft high.

This ZSU-57-2 manufactured before 1960 resides in a museum in Poland. *(Creative Commons Wisnia6522 via Wikimedia Commons)*

This ZSU-57-2 was destroyed in action near the South Vietnamese town of An Loc during the communist Easter Offensive in 1972. *(US Air Force)*

ZSU-23-4

Th ZSU-23-4 self-propelled antiaircraft gun remains in service with the Vietnamese Army. *(Creative Commons Hoangprs5 via Wikimedia Commons)*

T he tactic was simple and often effective: the North Vietnamese reasoned that the threat of their Soviet-supplied surface-to-air missiles (SAM) to American aircraft operating at high altitude would compel the pilots to drop to lower altitudes. When they did, it was expected these US aircraft would come within range of the quad-mounted 23mm anti-aircraft guns of the ZSU-23-4, nicknamed 'Shilka' after a river in southeastern Russia.

The ZSU-23-4, also nicknamed 'Zeus', served as the primary mobile close support air defence gun of the Soviet Red Army and numerous other countries for more than 30 years. Deployed to Vietnam sometime after 1972, it made a distinct impression on its adversaries. US Army evaluations of its capability bluntly stated that the ZSU-23-4's effectiveness indicated a 53% chance of hitting a target at altitude of 3,280ft with a 40-round burst of 23mm fire. During the last major campaign of the war in the spring of 1975, a 'Shilka' battery was known to have been fielded with the 237th Anti-Aircraft Artillery Regiment.

The system was at its deadliest moving forward in the field while supporting infantry advances and co-ordinating with Soviet surface-to-air missile systems such as the SA-6 Gainful and

This ZSU-23-4 is in the collection of the US Marine Corps at Camp Pendleton, California. *(US Marine Corps)*

The ZSU-23-4 entered service with the Red Army in 1965 as a replacement for the ZSU-57-2. *(US Army)*

SA-9 Gaskin. Its four 23mm AZP-23 water-cooled autocannon were enclosed in a welded turret with a 360° traverse and fired at a cyclical rate of up to 1,000 rounds per minute per gun. The gross rate of fire could reach 4,000 rounds per minute, coupled with the system's vertical range of just over 4,900ft that meant a veritable curtain of shells could be fired, posing a significant threat to low-flying fixed-wing aircraft and helicopters. The 23mm weapons were also capable of firing different types of ammunition independently.

The ZSU-23-4's GM-575 tracked vehicle chassis was derived from the PT-76 amphibious light tank. Although not identical, it shared may common components. Divided into three compartments, the chassis mounted the engine to the rear, the fighting compartment in the centre and the driver's section forward. The crew of four included a commander, gunner and radar operator. Personnel in the turret were protected somewhat from enemy fire by .33in of armour that could withstand

small-arms fire and shell fragments, while the maximum hull armour was about .36in thick.

Although the 'Shilka' was only lightly armoured and not amphibious, it was intended to keep pace with ground forces. Additionally, its 280hp, six-cylinder V-6R diesel engine, delivering a top speed of 27mph and range of 280 miles on improved roads, was underpowered in cross-country performance. While basic maintenance in the field was easily accomplished, certain electrical issues and availability of replacement engine components sometimes kept the 'Shilka' out of service for extended periods.

The 'Shilka' was designed during the late 1950s and early 1960s and was manufactured by the Mytishchi Engineering Works (MMZ) and the Ulyanovsk Mechanical Plant (UMZ). Between 1964 and 1982, more than 6,500 were produced, probably exceeding the numbers of any other vehicle of its type built in the Soviet Union. At one time, the Red Army alone had at least 2,000 examples serving with its frontline

This Iraqi 'Shilka' was destroyed by coalition forces during the 1991 Gulf War. *(US Department of Defense)*

Soldiers atop a ZSU-23-4, probably during the Soviet invasion of Afghanistan in the 1980s. *(Creative Commons Rettipai via Wikimedia Commons)*

anti-aircraft units. The vehicle weighed slightly less than 21 tons, stood just over 8½ft high and was over 10ft wide. Its development was undertaken in 1957 and it entered service in 1965 as a replacement for the ZSU-57-2 self-propelled anti-aircraft gun. Though it mounted a pair of powerful 57mm guns, the ZSU-57-2 could only carry 300 rounds, but the new ZSU-23-4 carried at least 2,000 rounds. Furthermore, the ZSU-57-2 was not capable of firing on the move and, due to the absence of radar, was considered rather inaccurate.

By contrast, one of the most distinctive features of the 'Shilka' was its RPK 2 Tobol radar. Known to Western nations as the 'gun dish', the Tobol was folded during travel and became a prominent feature of the ZSU-23-4 when deployed, raising the vehicle height to nearly 12ft. The RPK-2 was capable of acquiring targets at a distance of 12 miles and tracking them at 4.8 miles, although optical sighting and tracking were more effective against aircraft flying below 200ft.

When the radar was deployed in optimal conditions, the guns regularly engaged targets at a distance of just over two miles.

When necessary, the 'Shilka' was also used against ground targets, proving effective even against light armoured vehicles with its armour piercing ammunition. At the time of its introduction, it was perhaps better than an even match for any self-propelled anti-aircraft gun available to NATO. Its subsequent performance in the field precipitated some revisions in aerial combat tactics among NATO members.

Since 1972, the Vietnamese Army has maintained the 'Shilka' in its anti-aircraft inventory and upgraded the system periodically. In addition to its Vietnam service, the ZSU-23-4 was prominently utilised by Egyptian forces during the 1973 Yom Kippur War and was credited with shooting down a number of Israeli aircraft that had descended to lower altitude to elude Egyptian SAMs. Through the years of the Cold War, the 'Shilka' was exported to more than 20 Warsaw Pact countries and several other client states of the Soviet Union. ■

ZSU-23-4 displayed in a museum in Smolensk, Russia. *(Creative Commons Vitaly V. Kuzmin)*

BM-21

Vietnamese BM-21 Grad mobile rocket launchers fire their 122mm rockets amid thick vegetation.
(Creative Commons Hoangprs5 via Wikimedia Commons)

launcher. In its place, the BM-21 combined the 122mm M-21OF rocket and launcher with the Ural 375D 6X6 truck chassis. With the missile system aboard, the truck's 180hp V-8 engine delivered a top road speed of 47mph and a range of 470 miles.

Development of the BM-21 began in May 1960 with Resolution 578-236 adopted by the Soviet Council of Ministers, and instruction centred on the installation of the rocket system aboard a readily available vehicle. Testing began in late 1961 and, with the endorsement of the Red Army, production began in 1964, with more than 8,000 built to date. Designed to provide general fire support, systems such as the BM-21 have a long history of effectiveness against opposing infantry, armour and other tactical targets.

Attached to the flatbed of the Ural truck, the system consists of a rectangular arrangement of 40 tubes, with the entire apparatus capable of turning to avoid damage to the unprotected cab of the vehicle from the blast of a launch. The system is manned by a crew of three or four and the rockets may be fired in separate salvoes, individually or in a single launch either from inside the

During World War Two, one of the most effective Red Army weapons on the Eastern Front was the series of multiple launch rocket systems (MLRS) collectively nicknamed 'Katyusha', which translates as 'Little Kate'. These were highly mobile systems that allowed a volume of rocket fire, then the rapid relocation of the truck-based weapon to elude enemy counter-fire.

Although the BM-21 Grad (in Russian, BM is the acronym for 'combat vehicle', while Grad translates as 'hailstorm') was developed some years after the 1939-1945 conflict ended, it was influenced by the Soviet experience in the Great Patriotic War and is often colloquially described as 'Katyusha' as well.

During the early years of the Cold War, it was logical for the Soviet military establishment to continue to modernise its MLRS capability. The BM-21 was developed in the early 1960s as a replacement for the outdated BM-14, which mounted a 140mm rocket

This BM-21 grad launch system shows the configuration of missile tubes aboard the truck.
(Creative Commons Dmitry A. Mottl via Wikimedia Commons)

Crews prepare a battery of six BM-21 Grad missile systems for firing. *(US Department of Defense)*

cab or via a cable stretching up to 210ft. Preparatory activities can be completed by an experienced crew in as little as three minutes and the rockets can be launched at a rate of two per second or the entire complement in about 20 seconds. The rockets are nearly 9½ft long and deliver a variety of warheads with a range of approximately 12 miles.

The BM-21 was first used in action by the Red Army during a 1969 border clash with troops of the People's Republic of China. In Vietnam, the North Vietnamese Army and Viet Cong referred to the BM-21 as the DKZ-B and used a man-portable single-round tripod-launched version called the Grad P that was originally designed by the Soviets as a Special Forces weapon. Vietnam is believed to have retained more than 700 BM-14 and BM-21 systems. ∎

BM-31-12

This Russian memorial includes a BM-31-12and Soviet-built ZIS truck. *(Creative Commons High Contrast via Wikimedia Commons)*

Among the enduring images of World War Two on the Eastern Front are those of the Red Army's powerful 'Katyusha' rockets streaking from their truck-borne launchers toward distant Nazi targets. This concept of mobile rocket artillery was brought forward in the 1930s, and during the Great Patriotic War the Soviets became acknowledged experts in the use of rockets in tactical military operations.

When the rockets were first used in combat, they came as a rude surprise to the German forces and they were given the grudgingly respectful nickname of 'Stalin's Organs'. The 'Katyusha' rockets were originally intended for use aboard attack aircraft, but in 1938 the weapons were tested with mobile ground launchers. Three years later, the first system of its kind, the BM-13, entered production. The high explosive rockets that the systems fired were not precision weapons, but rather intended to saturate an area with a volume of fire that would devastate enemy troop concentrations, armour and light vehicles.

The truck-borne missile systems were mounted on the flatbeds of 4X4 and 6X6 vehicles made by Soviet manufacturers and the American 2½-ton 6X6 Studebaker US6 truck obtained through Lend-Lease. The rockets themselves ranged in size from 82mm to 300mm and could be fired individually, in clusters or in full salvoes, with a battery of 'Katyusha' rockets easily saturating a target with overwhelming firepower. More than 10,000 'Katyusha' platforms were built during the course of World War Two and many of these have been upgraded and remained operational with the Red Army, Soviet Bloc nations and client states such as North Korea and North Vietnam for decades.

The first 'Katyushas' went into action against the Nazis in the summer of 1941. By the spring of 1944, the SKB 'Compressor' Design Bureau had paired the Studebaker truck with a launch system carrying 12 300mm rockets. In addition to its debut in the Great Patriotic War, the so-called BM-31-12 was also used

A BM-31-12 rocket system and Studebaker truck during the World War Two victory parade in Moscow, 1945. *(Creative Commons Ministry of Defence of the Russian Federation via Wikimedia Commons)*

by communist forces in Vietnam. Following conventional Soviet nomenclature, 'BM' represented a ground vehicle, '31' indicated the type of rocket used and '12' the number of rails or tubes mounted. The 'Katyusha' first appeared with North Vietnamese forces in 1966, and the Vietnamese Army has maintained and upgraded its inventory of the system ever since.

The early success of the BM-13 mobile rocket launcher spurred the Red Army's request for a heavier weapon system. The M-30 rocket with a range of 3,100 yards was originally evaluated, but gave way to the longer-range M-31 and M-31-UK capable of reaching o4,730 yards and 4,400 yards respectively. In action during the Soviet offensive of 1944-1945, the BM-31-12 proved quite effective, particularly during the urban fighting in the German capital of Berlin, where its heavy firepower levelled buildings and strongpoints with saturation salvoes.

The BM-31-12 constituted an improved version of the 'Katyusha', including a welded launch apparatus, new electronics and better overall operating characteristics for the unguided missile launch process. Upper and lower crossbars were added to secure the missiles on their rails during transport and to prevent spontaneous ignition when the vehicle was in a secure location. Testing revealed a stable platform that was fired either from within the Studebaker's cab or from outside. The new technology had broad applications in rocket launch technology that stretched beyond that of the tactical BM-31-12.

The BM-31-12, also known as 'Andryusha' or 'Andrew', entered service with the Red Army in April 1944 and became the main launching system for the M-31 and M-31-UK 300mm rockets with warheads weighing 64lb. After World War Two, the rocket system was also mounted aboard the modified chassis of the ZIS-151 6X6 truck built by Automotive Factory No. 2 Zavod imeni Stalina (ZIS).

The BM-31-12 was capable of firing a full salvo of 12 rounds in 15-20 seconds. Approximately

A Red Army BM-31-12 crew prepares the system for launch during combat on a Berlin street in 1945. *(TASS Georgy Ugrinovich)*

BM-31-12 displayed in the Artillery Museum in St Petersburg, Russia. *(Creative Commons Damien via Wikimedia Commons)*

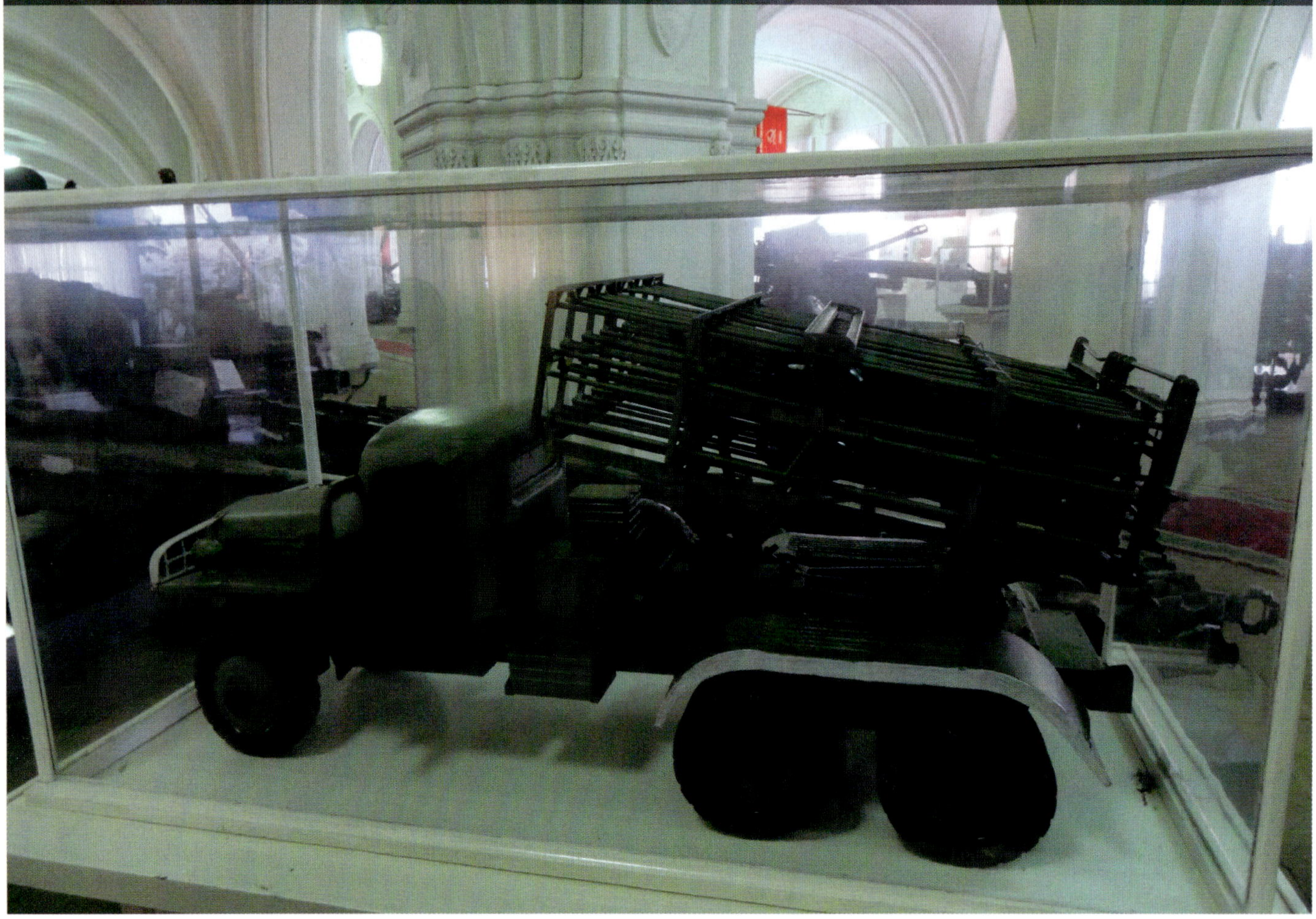

15 minutes were required to reload and recharge the system, but the vehicle itself was vulnerable to artillery counter-battery fire, as well as US and South Vietnamese air assets since the act of firing produced a substantial smoke signature. Therefore, the system was regularly required to displace immediately after launching. The 'Katyusha' rockets were effective terror weapons as well, sometimes being directed toward civilian population centres or fired from stand-off distances against US forward combat bases. Viet Cong guerrillas also used a single-tube man portable variant of the lighter rockets to launch nocturnal harassing attacks against US and South Vietnamese installations, then melt away into the darkness.

The Studebaker truck was powered by the 95hp, six-cylinder Hercules petrol engine delivering a top speed of just over 40mph with a range of 236 miles.

Along with the Vietnamese Army, the 'Katyusha' family of rockets remains a frontline weapon for many military forces around the world. It has also become a prominent weapon in the ongoing conflicts in the Middle East with Hezbollah and Hamas frequently using them to fire on targets in Israel from Gaza and across the Israeli border. ■

High ground clearance was a positive attribute of the Studebaker truck for BM-31-12 operations. *(Creative Commons ShinePhantom via Wikimedia Commons)*

The launch apparatus of the BM-31-12 offered improvements over earlier 'Katyusha' models. *(Creative Commons ShinePhantom via Wikimedia Commons)*

BTR-40

A Soviet BTR-40 in a Budapest street during the 1956 Hungarian uprising. *(Creative Commons Pesti Srác2 Via Wikimedia Commons)*

The BTR-40 was an early Soviet attempt to combine reconnaissance and troop transport capabilities. *(Creative Commons Hans Kloss via Wikimedia Commons)*

T he Soviet armed forces gained an appreciation for mobility during the course of World War Two and leaned heavily on the fast and reliable BT-64 armoured car for reconnaissance and scouting duties. However, when the war was over, the requirement was for a new vehicle, capable of transporting troops across waterways and difficult terrain while also performing reconnaissance.

The BT-64 was produced through 1946 and more than 9,000 were eventually built, but soon after its run was completed the initiative to produce a successor had already experienced some setbacks at the Gorky Automobile Plant (GAZ), where VA Dedkov was serving as chief engineer for the project. GAZ had built two prototypes by 1947, and both had been rejected. By 1950, another pair of test vehicles emerged. Influenced by the design of the GAZ 63 four-wheel-drive truck that had entered production in 1946, the new BTR-40 and BTR-40A were introduced.

The BTR-40 prototypes differed in their anticipated roles. The BTR-40 was planned with machine gun armament as an option, while the BTR-40A was intended for anti-aircraft defence with a pair of 14.5mm KPVT heavy machine guns in a traversing turret. Both vehicles used the chassis and other components from the GAZ 63, including the 80hp, six-cylinder GAZ 40 petrol engine that produced a top road speed of nearly 50mph and a range of 267 miles. The vehicle weighed just shy of six tons, stood just over 7ft high and was more than 16ft long.

The design of the BTR-40 allowed the driver and passenger to enter and exit through cab doors, while the rear accommodated up to eight combat troops or just over a single ton of cargo. The box-like rear section was only lightly armoured at a maximum of .33in, providing protection against small arms or shell fragments. Reports indicate that the common US .50-calibre Browning machine gun round was capable of penetrating the thin skin. The rear of the vehicle was open-topped and sometimes covered with a canvas tarpaulin for protection from the elements. Although the basic BTR-40 was often unarmed, mounts were provided for up to three 7.62mm light machine guns and two firing ports were located on either side of the hull for infantry use from within the vehicle.

The BTR-40's field performance demonstrated a deficiency in cross country operations, particularly when fording streams. By 1954, an amphibious modification was undertaken, later transitioning into an amphibious scout car designated the BTR-40P or BRDM-1.

The BTR-40 in numerous variants was produced from 1950 to 1960, with approximately 8,500 built. It provided adequate overall performance in the reconnaissance, troop transport, command and communications roles, serving concurrently for a time with its intended replacement, the BTR-152. It was also widely exported and utilised by communist forces throughout the Vietnam conflict. ◼

This BTR-40 has been upgraded and serves today with security forces in Indonesia. *(Kodim 0726/ Sukoharjo (Military District Command 0726 Sukoharjo))*

BTR-50

A BTR-50 crew puts its vehicle through training in 2018, demonstrating the longevity of the APC. *(Creative Commons Adam Hauner via Wikimedia Commons)*

East German soldiers work with a BTR-50 variant near a waterway in 1968. *(Creative Commons Bybbisch94, Christian Gebhardt via Wikimedia Commons)*

In the early 1950s, the Soviet armed forces maintained two wheeled armoured personnel carriers (APCs): the BTR-40 and the BTR-152. While both were intended for cross-country performance, they were deemed inadequate when it came to amphibious characteristics and could handle only shallow rivers and streams. Designers at the Chelyabinsk Tank Plant VNII-100 Institute (ChTz) near Leningrad, the same facility that had developed the PT-76 light amphibious tank, proposed their vehicle serve as the basis for a tracked APC that would produce the desired capabilities.

Developed as Object 750, the prototype BTR-50 was put through lengthy trials beginning in 1952 and approved for production two years later. It was not seen in public until the Red Army parades and functions in 1957. The vehicle remained in production in the Soviet Union until 1970 and continued for two more years in Czechoslovakia, with more than 6,000 units built in numerous variants and upgrades.

From the late 1950s to the 1970s, the BTR-50 was exported to Warsaw Pact countries and Soviet client states. It remains in service with many nations today, but was retired from the Red Army in the 1970s in favour of the BMP-1 infantry fighting vehicle (IFV).

During the Vietnam war, the North Vietnamese government made substantial requests of the Soviet Union for arms and armaments. By 1965, a total of 50 PT-76 light tanks and 50 BTR-50 APCs had been received. The BTR-50 was already considered by some as outmoded despite its subsequent longevity. The tropical climate and the diversity of terrain truly tested the APC in circumstances that were quite different to the rolling plains of Eastern and Central Europe where it was originally intended to operate. Swamps, river deltas, rice paddies, mountains and plains were challenging, but performance was improved over wheeled alternatives. The BTR-50 was attractive due to the economies of scale derived from common components with the PT-76, while its cost savings and reliability in the field boosted its service life.

At the same time, the BTR-50 was often unarmed, thus was at a distinct disadvantage when caught in the open during a firefight rather than serving as a simple 'battle taxi', delivering its complement of 10 fully loaded combat infantrymen and then vacating the area. Its armour varied from about ½in forward on the hull to just over ¼in to the rear, which was ineffective against anything but small-arms fire and shell fragments. It was said that the rounds of the US .50-calibre Browning M2 machine gun could penetrate the thin skin of the BTR-50.

Three BTR-50s were converted in the field in Vietnam to self-propelled anti-aircraft guns by mounting a pair of ZPU 14.5mm heavy machine guns for the 202nd Motorized Infantry Regiment. These saw action during fighting in Quang Tri Province in 1973 and 1975 near the end of the conflict. One of the converted vehicles, BTR-609, was captured by US forces in the battle at My Chanh in the spring of 1973.

The basic BTR-50 shared similar characteristics with its parent, the PT-76, with both utilising the same boat-like chassis intended for amphibious operations. The engine was identical as well. Positioned at the rear, the 240hp V-6 petrol powerplant produced a top speed on improved roads of just over 27mph and a range of 249 miles. The same pair of bilge pumps and water jets at the rear of the vehicle were engaged to cross waterways with a top speed of nearly 7mph.

Soviet armoured vehicles, including the BTR-50, during the May Day parade in Moscow on May 1, 1964. *(Creative Commons Thomas Taylor Hammond Collection University of Virginia Center for Russian, East European, and Eurasian Studies via Wikimedia Commons)*

BTR-50s of the Finnish Army being loaded aboard rail cars. *(Creative Commons Methem via Wikimedia Commons)*

The two-man crew sat forward, with the driver at centre and commander to the left. The open-topped passenger compartment was located in the centre of the vehicle, with benches for seating, and soldiers entering and exiting by climbing over the sides. The BTR-50 stood 6 ½ft high, was just over 10ft wide and stretched more than 23ft long. Two pistol ports were located on either side of the vehicle to allow soldiers to fight from inside and, at times, there were pintle-mounted 7.62mm machine guns fixed to the vehicle.

Some notable improvements were made to the basic BTR-50 during its early years of operation. Pintle mounts were installed for the heavy KPV 14.5mm machine gun in 1954, and this variant was designated the BTR-50PA. In 1958, the BTR-50PJ was introduced with a fully enclosed armour roof that was accessed by a pair of large rectangular hatches on the sides and a third hatch toward the front. Although an awareness of the need for defence against nuclear, biological, and chemical (NBC) weapons was emerging, this variant did not provide for these, although a pair of ventilators were installed.

The BTR-50PN command vehicle entered service in 1958, equipped with three radios, while an improved command vehicle, the BTR-

A Syrian BTR-50 destroyed during fighting in the Golan Heights during the 1973 Yom Kippur War. *(US Central Intelligence Agency)*

50PU, became available a year later. Operated by a crew of 10, the latter vehicle was often built with bay projections toward the front.

The BTR-50 became a template for the further evolution of the APC and genesis of the dedicated infantry fighting vehicle (IFV). Although wheeled vehicles would again be employed for ease of field maintenance and higher speed, the BTR-50 is recognised as one of the best-known vehicles of its kind produced in the 20th Century. ∎

A BTR-50 on display at the Jaisalmer War Museum in Rajasthan, India. *(Creative Commons Savanv10 via Wikimedia Commons)*

SUBSCRIBE TODAY!

Classic Military Vehicle is the best-selling publication in the UK dedicated to the coverage of all historic military vehicles.

/collections/subscriptions

Free 2nd class P&P on BFPO orders. Overseas charges apply.

BTR-60

A BTR-60 with cone-shaped turret and heavy machine gun. *(Creative Commons Billyhill via Wikimedia Commons)*

The Soviet military establishment authorised two design bureaus, Gorkovsky Avtomobilny Zavod (GAZ) and ZIL of the Likhachev Moscow Automobile Plant, to produce a heavy APC for the mechanisation of troops assigned to tank divisions and a lighter vehicle for motorised infantry divisions. The former led to the introduction of the BMP-1 infantry fighting vehicle (IFV), while the latter would produce the BTR-60.

Engineer VA Dedkov led GAZ engineering work on the new light APC beginning in the winter of 1956, initially producing early designs that failed to incorporate the armoured roof or the need for protection against nuclear, biological and chemical weapons (NBC) that the Red Army had specified. By 1959, a competition was held between the latest GAZ prototype and those of the ZIL and KAZ bureaus, which had subsequently joined the research effort. Interestingly, Soviet documents suggest that the GAZ vehicle did not perform as well as the KAZ Object 1015, but it was nevertheless chosen for production in 1960 due to lower cost and simplicity of construction.

While the obvious deficiency of an open top was not corrected in the original production BTR-60P, it was in the improved BTR-60PA, ordered from 1963 onward. The 8X8 BTR-60 weighed nearly 11½ tons, stood more than 7½ft high and was nearly 25ft long. Its powerplant included a pair of 90hp, six-cylinder GAZ-49B petrol engines producing a top road speed of 50mph and a range of 300 miles. The twin engines functioned independently from one another, so if one were disabled, the other could still move the vehicle. The amphibious capability of the BTR-60 was provided, with the engagement of a centrally mounted jet at the rear of the vehicle, but this arrangement frequently proved unreliable. The welded steel armour protection ranged from .2in to .35in on the hull.

From 1965, the BTR-60PAI featured the addition of a cone-shaped BPU-1 turret adapted from that of the BPRM-2 amphibious armoured car. The turret was protected by .29in of steel armour and accommodated a 14.5mm heavy machine gun for defence against low-flying aircraft or close

The post-World War Two requirement for a dedicated Red Army armoured personnel carrier (APC) led to the development of the BTR-40 and BTR-152, both open-topped vehicles. By the early 1950s, the BTR-40 was soon oriented toward reconnaissance, while the BTR-152 became the primary Soviet-built APC. While these types marked milestones in the evolution of Soviet combat troop transport, neither addressed the need for a fully enclosed APC that would offer reasonable protection against enemy small-arms fire and shell fragments.

The shortcomings of both the BTR-40 and the BTR-152 in battle were laid bare during the Suez Crisis of 1956, when Egyptian Army vehicles suffered heavy losses, often due to indirect fire, and the Hungarian Uprising in the same year, when Soviet troops were killed or wounded after their APCs were targeted with rifle and machine gun fire, hand grenades and homemade Molotov cocktails in the street of Budapest.

Open-topped BTR-60s parade through Moscow on May Day in 1964. *(Creative Commons Thomas Taylor Hammond University of Virginia Center for Russian, East European, and Eurasian Studies via Wikimedia Commons)*

A combat loaded BTR-60P crosses rugged terrain during a training exercise. *(US Department of Defense)*

new vehicle in 1961 and they appeared with North Vietnamese forces in 1966, serving for the duration of the conflict. They were also deployed by Soviet forces during the 1968 Prague Spring uprising in Czechoslovakia and engaged the Chinese People's Liberation Army during the border dispute of 1969.

In the battle of Damansky Island, the BTR-60 was prominent in the Soviet expulsion of Chinese troops from the contested area, although it was susceptible to the shoulder-fired rocket-propelled grenades carried by Chinese soldiers. This experience confirmed for Soviet armour designers a demarcation between APCs that primarily served as 'battle taxis', delivering troops to the vicinity of an engagement and then withdrawing, and close combat IFVs. In fact, the Soviets had been working to produce their IFVs for several years and a few of the new BMP-1 design, which entered service in 1966, were present during the Sino-Soviet border battles. ■

combat against enemy infantry, along with a coaxially-mounted 7.62mm light machine gun.

The protective roof fitted to the BTR-60PA reduced the troop-carrying capacity of the vehicle from 16 combat ready soldiers to 14, while some sources state troop capacities were as low as seven. An estimated 27,000 vehicles were built by 1990, including those produced in the Soviet Union into the mid-1970s and others built in Romania, a Soviet Bloc country, through 1990. Variants included command, communications, mortar carrier, artillery fire direction types and others.

The BTR-60 layout was a departure from earlier vehicles, with the engine compartment to the rear, requiring the troops to enter and exit the vehicle through the sides or roof hatches assisted by a pair of steps on each side of the hull. The crew of two was located forward, with the driver seated to the left and the commander on the right. Later variants also included a gunner positioned to operate the turreted machine guns.

The first BTR-60s were delivered to the Red Army in 1960, supplanting the BTR-152 as the primary APC. Western observers first saw the

Soviet soldiers pose with their BTR-60 in the 1980s. *(Creative Commons Союз Ветеранов военнослужащих проходящих службу в Сирии via Wikimedia Commons)*

A relic of Soviet military involvement in Afghanistan, this BTR-60 lies derelict and rusting. *(US Marine Corps)*

BTR-60PA on display at a museum in Russia. *(ProDiman Public Domain)*

BTR-152

Newsreel footage and still photographs of Red Army soldiers riding into battle atop the T-34 medium tank are iconic images of World War Two on the Eastern Front. Rapid mobility was a key element of mutual support as infantry and armour advanced toward Berlin. However, infantrymen were often exposed to enemy small-arms and artillery fire in such positions.

Experience with the US-supplied M3 Halftrack and evaluation of captured German types gave rise to the development of a Soviet armoured personnel carrier (APC) that would allow infantry to keep pace with rapidly advancing armoured formations with a modicum of protection. In the wake of the Great Patriotic War, the Gorkovsky Avtomobilny Zavod (GAZ) Design Bureau was established to produce a Soviet APC, wheeled and capable of carrying eight combat troops. The initial result, the BTR-40, was accepted into service, but was generally not used in the APC role due to its size limitations.

Concurrent with the development of the BTR-40, the Zavod Imeni Stalina (ZIS) design bureau in Moscow worked on the prototype of the BTR-152 under the direction of engineer Boris Fitterman. The chassis of a Zwas-151 truck was the basis of the new 6X6 vehicle and sloped armour protection was added, ranging from .16in on the underside to .59in forward. After early testing revealed lacklustre cross-country performance, a series of more powerful engines were introduced, including the 110hp, six-cylinder ZIL-137K petrol powerplant that generated a top road speed of nearly 47mph and a range of 404 miles.

Testing concluded in December 1949 and the BTR-152 was accepted into Red Army service the following spring. Western observers saw the first example during a military parade in Moscow in 1951. The vehicle was constantly upgraded and modified through a production run that ended in 1960, with approximately 15,000 examples completed, including some manufactured as unlicensed copies in the People's Republic of China. As the first true Soviet-designed APC, the BTR-152 became the workhorse of troop transport for the Red Army, while the BTR-40 entered production in late 1950 and served primarily as a reconnaissance vehicle.

The Soviet BTR-152 bears some resemblance to US and German troop transporters of World War Two. *(Creative Commons LutzBruno via Wikimedia Commons)*

This BTR-152 was destroyed in Budapest during street fighting in the Hungarian Uprising of 1956. *(Creative Commons Nagy Gyula via Wikimedia Commons)*

BTR-152 APCs proceed along Manezhnaya Square in Moscow during the funeral of Premier Josef Stalin on March 9, 1953. *(US Government)*

Like other early APCs, the passenger compartment of the BTR-152 was open-topped, exposing occupants to some enemy fire. It was capable of carrying up to 18 fully equipped combat troops and was serviced by a driver and commander seated forward. The BTR-152 stood more than 6½ft high, was over 22ft long and weighed nearly 10 tons. Armament included a fully traversing mount for either a 7.62mm light machine gun or 12.7mm anti-aircraft machine gun.

Although cost effective, the cross-country performance of the BTR-152 was disappointing. Even as it became the primary vehicle of its kind in Soviet service, work was proceeding on a series of 8X8 vehicles.

The BTR-152 was exported to numerous countries, including North Vietnam, which utilised it during offensive operations as early as 1965 and continues to field an upgraded version today. ∎

TYPE 63 APC

A Viet Cong flag flies from a Type 63 near the town of Phan Thiet, South Vietnam, during the Spring Offensive of 1975. *(Creative Commons tommy japan via Wikimedia Commons)*

The first armoured vehicle of any type constructed in the People's Republic of China without direct influence from Soviet engineers or duplication of a Soviet vehicle, the Type 63 armoured personnel carrier (APC) was supplied to the North Vietnamese in the latter stages of the Vietnam war , then used against them during the border clashes between China and Vietnam in the late 1970s.

The Type 63 came about with the Chinese government's issuing of a nationwide "scientific and strategic plan" to develop a tracked APC in the summer of 1958, with mass production to begin by 1960. Tasked with the project, designers at the No. 1 Specialized Institute of the First Machinery Works, where some engineers with experience in armoured vehicle design were already employed, began preliminary development. Technicians of the Harbin Engineering Academy were also involved, under the direction of the scientific department of the People's Liberation Army armoured command along with the Fifth Department of First Machinery Works. Apparently, some Soviet advisers were involved in the initial design work, but their input has not been deemed sufficient to undermine the premise that the Type 63, with its industrial designation of YW531, was developed by the Chinese alone. Manufacturing was undertaken by the Yong Ding Machinery Factory, which later became a subsidiary of NORINCO (China North Industries Group Corporation).

The Type 63 incorporated some features and components of other light vehicles. Through a production run that lasted into the 1980s, approximately 8,000 were built in 17 variants, more than any other APC except for the US M113

Designed in China without direct Soviet influence, the Type 63 APC reached North Vietnam late in the conflict. *(Creative Commons Max Smith via Wikimedia Commons)*

and Soviet BMP series. The Type 63 was built for People's Liberation Army use and also for export.

The hull of the amphibious APC was fully welded, with an angular forward section. Its cold steel rolled homogenous armour was thickest in front at slightly more than ½in. In other areas, thickness varied to nearly ⅓in, providing reasonable protection against most small-arms fire. The vehicle weighed nearly 14 tons fully loaded, stood nearly 8½ft high and was nearly 18ft long. A crew of two, a commander and driver, sat forward to the right and left respectively, with a seat behind the driver to accommodate a third crewmember if necessary. Up to 10 fully equipped combat troops occupied the transport compartment to the rear, with entry or exit through large doors at the back or a pair of hatches in the roof.

The APC was powered by the 260hp, eight-cylinder NORINCO Type 615OL diesel engine with a top speed of 40mph on the road and a range of 311 miles. Export versions of the Type 63 were regularly equipped with a 320hp Deutz/KHD BF8L 413F diesel engine. Standard armament consisted of a single Chinese Type 54 12.7mm machine gun in an open mount on the roof. ■

The boat-like hull of the Type 63 APC is visible in this photo of a museum piece. *(Creative Commons People's Liberation Army Tank Museum via Wikimedia Commons)*

The MTU-20 AVLB was constructed atop the chassis of a T-55 main battle tank. *(Creative Commons Richard Allen via Wikimedia Commons)*

The mobile MTU-20 AVLB was folded in transport and extended at both ends during deployment. *(Creative Commons Bukvoed via Wikimedia Commons)*

MTU-20

In the spring of 1955, both the burgeoning NATO alliance and the Soviet Union and its Eastern European client states that formed the basis of the Warsaw Pact prepared for an anticipated renewal of hostilities: a land war in Europe. While such preparations seemed logical, some of the weaponry developed in the Cold War era was distributed to hotspots around the world.

Global tensions sometimes erupted into proxy wars as the US and Soviet superpowers sponsored opposing sides with financial and diplomatic support, military hardware and, at times, boots on the ground. Such was the case in Korea and Vietnam, where communist and ostensibly democratic armies, guerrillas and militias came into conflict. While the Soviet Union did send military advisers to North Vietnam, their numbers were dwarfed by the size of the US troop commitment of more than 500,000.

The Soviet government supplied North Vietnam with various military systems designed for battle or supply and logistics functions. One of these was the MTU-20 armoured vehicle launched bridge (AVLB). During its assessment of tactical combat that might occur in Europe, Red Army war planners determined that roughly 65% of the rivers and streams they might encounter during a westward advance were no wider than 20-25 yards, thus an early emphasis on tracked vehicles that could quickly deploy bridges was pursued.

By 1957, a few AVLB vehicles had been tested and entered service with the bridging apparatus affixed to the chassis of the T-34 medium tank. Overlapping that development, the design of a purpose-built AVLB was underway by the middle of the decade. The MTU-54 AVLB, sometimes referred to as the MTU-1, made its debut with the Red Army in 1955, carrying a bridge was that situated horizontally atop the chassis and stretched nearly 13½ yards. While the bridge did not fold, a chain system moved it forward to deploy and could span a waterway or ground depression of 12 yards with a load-bearing limit of just over 55 tons.

By the mid-1960s, the MTU-54 had largely been replaced by the MTU-20, mounted aboard the chassis of a T55 main battle tank. The 24-yard bridge works were folded from either end in transit to allow for a longer span, which crossed nearly 20 yards in full deployment with a load capacity of just over 66 tons. Its deployment and recovery time were remarkably rapid at five minutes and seven minutes respectively.

The notable MTU-20 advances over the MTU-54 included a snorkel for traversing waterways, stabilisers for a more secure set-up, an automatic onboard fire suppression system and defences against nuclear, biological and chemical weapons, a feature that had become more commonplace by the time of the MTU-20's introduction in 1967. ■

MTU-20 shown in service with the Israeli armed forces during the 1973 Yom Kippur War. *(Creative Commons National Library of Israel via Wikimedia Commons)*

GAZ-51/63

GAZ-51 2½-ton general purpose truck on display in a military museum in Belarus. *(Creative Commons Guomundur D. Haraldsson via Wikimedia Commons)*

In the mid-1930s, some time before the Red Army embarked on its conquest of eastern Poland in 1939 and the Soviet Union was invaded by its former ally Germany in June 1941, engineers at the Gorkovsky Avtomobilny Zavod (GAZ) design bureau were hard at work developing a general purpose truck for the Soviet military.

GAZ began using a readily available chassis based on a design originated with the US Ford Motor Company in 1937 and produced a prototype in the spring of 1939. Evaluations were completed by June 1940 and GAZ leaders were pleased to showcase their new vehicle at an agricultural exhibition in Moscow that year. Although plans for mass production proceeded in the following months, the Nazi invasion of the Soviet Union interrupted that schedule.

Components originally intended for the GAZ-51 were diverted to other vehicle types and production ceased until 1943. In that year, the resumption of 2X4 GAZ-51 trucks was accompanied by the re-energised development of the GAZ-63, a virtually identical vehicle with 4X4 capability. The GAZ-51/63 pair were produced toward the end of World War Two in limited numbers.

During the period of interruption, GAZ chief designer AD Prosvirnin had introduced several modifications to the original vehicle, including an adapted cab based on the Studebaker US6, which was familiar in the Soviet Union through Lend-Lease. Technical revisions were included and the standard capacity was increased from 2 to 2½ tons.

The first production GAZ-51s were delivered to the Red Army in late 1945 and production increased to more than 3,100 the following year. In 1958, production peaked at more than 173,000 and the run concluded in the Soviet Union in April 1975, with estimates of total completed vehicles approaching 3.5 million in all variants, including dump trucks, ambulances, communications and others. The type was also produced in Poland.

Decorated GAZ-51 truck with sides down during a 1964 parade. *(Creative Commons Morvay Kinga via Wikimedia Commons)*

The GAZ-51/63 was exported to several countries, including North Vietnam, where the Soviet Union supplied roughly half of the trucks received between 1965 and 1971. The GAZ-51/63 was powered by the 70hp, six-cylinder GAZ-51 engine, an improved version of the earlier GAZ-11, which was derived from the license-built Dodge D5 powerplant.

Its top road speed was 30mph and its range was 500 miles. Further modifications to the overall vehicle were instituted in the 1950s under the direction of designer BI Shikhov.

The GAZ-63 was showcased to Kremlin dignitaries in 1945 and entered production in the autumn of 1948. More than 470,000 of the 4X4 version were built. ∎

This 4X4 GAZ-63 at a museum in The Netherlands has a winch attached to the front bumper. *(Creative Commons AlfvanBeem via Wikimedia Commons)*

GAZ-69

A 1958 GAZ-69 with canvas cover. *(Creative Commons Alf van Beem via Wikimedia Commons)*

During the Great Patriotic War, the Soviet Union received more than 40,000 examples of the American Jeep through the Lend-Lease programme and the Red Army came to appreciate the characteristics of the rugged US-built, four-wheel-drive light truck in its various iterations. However, Soviet military vehicle engineers had been working on all-wheel-drive capability since the 1930s, progressing in performance with each new design.

Through the course of World War Two, the GAZ-61, GAZ-64 and GAZ-67 had been produced, while the Soviets leaned heavily on their US imports. After the war ended, the Gorkovsky Avtomobilny Zavod (GAZ) design bureau continued its work on a succeeding generation of domestically produced light 4X4 trucks. The GAZ-69 development was led by a team under the direction of engineer Grigoriy Vasserman, with one of the immediate requirements being more favourable fuel consumption than its immediate predecessor, the GAZ-67B.

While earlier light trucks had been developed in a matter of weeks due to the urgencies of war, the evolution of the GAZ-69 was a slower and more deliberate process. Undertaken in 1946, the effort yielded its first prototype, nicknamed 'Truzhenik' or 'Toiler' a year later. These were dispatched across the Soviet Union and put through extensive field testing in the country's varied terrain, with test crews logging more than 62,000 miles in some of the prototypes. Nevertheless, production was not approved for some time and was finally authorised on August 25, 1953.

During a production run that lasted until 1972 in the Soviet Union and 1975 by ARO (Auto Romania) in Romania, more than 600,000 GAZ-69 offroad vehicles were completed. By the mid-1950s, the GAZ-69 was replacing the wartime GAZ-67 and the surviving, extensively used American Jeeps that remained in service. It became the primary vehicle of its type for the Red Army during the Cold War and was delivered to many client states, including North Vietnam.

The GAZ-69 carried eight passengers, including the driver, or 1,100 pounds of cargo or varied combinations of the two. It weighed 1¾ tons, stretched more than 12½ft long and was nearly 6½ft high. Its 55hp, four-cylinder petrol engine produced a top road speed of 56mph; later, more powerful 65hp engines pushed top speed to 62mph.

The base vehicle included standard entry and exit doors forward, with a folding bench on either side to the rear. A four-door version, the GAZ-69A, was also built. A folding canvas top was available and the type was also built for civilian use, although these were required to meet military performance standards in case they were requisitioned in wartime. ■

GAZ-69A parked on a city street in East Berlin in 1966. *(Creative Commons Brian Harrington Spier via Wikimedia Commons)*

Red Army soldiers in GAZ-69s during the Moscow May Day parade of 1964. *(Creative Commons Thomas Taylor Hammond University of Virginia Center for Russian, East European, and Eurasian Studies via Wikimedia Commons)*

An IFA W 50 medium duty truck crosses a rain-swollen river in Vietnam. *(Creative Commons Stas Kulesh via Wikimedia Commons)*

IFA W 50

A highly-classified US government report from February 1972 stated that thousands of North Vietnamese trucks had been destroyed during attacks on the Ho Chi Minh Trail. American aircraft and South Vietnamese anti-guerrilla ground operations aimed at interdicting communist supplies and infiltration had led to the losses. However, the report also stated that the losses had since been replaced and then some: "The truck inventories currently maintained in North Vietnam are about double the levels maintained in the early years of the war." The USAF reported that it had destroyed 18,000 trucks and damaged another 7,000 in 1971 alone, so the ability of the

North Vietnamese to replenish their inventory is nothing short of astounding. According to the US report, Eastern European countries of the Soviet Bloc supplied roughly 25% of the trucks imported by North Vietnam between 1965 and 1971, numbering approximately 9,500 units.

One of the steadiest suppliers of transport vehicles to North Vietnam outside the Soviet Union was the German Democratic Republic, more commonly known as East Germany. The medium duty IFA W 50 was one of the most prominent vehicles. While the Soviet Union purchased its share of IFA W 50s, many were shipped overseas to Southeast Asia, Africa and South America.

During the late 1950s, the Kraftfahrzeugwerk Ernst Grube Werdau initiated design work to replace earlier truck models. Specifications for a new type included a hauling capacity of nearly five tons with all-wheel-drive capability. An original cab-over prototype designated the S4500 was delivered in 1959. Meanwhile, specifications were altered to raise hauling capacity to 5½ tons. Subsequently, the designation was changed to W for Werdau and 50 to designate a 5-ton capacity. In December 1962, the East German government decided to award the production contract to VEB Industriewerke Ludwigsfelde.

In the spring of 1963, the IFA industrial conglomerate began building a factory for the production of the IFA W 50 in the city of

Ludwigsfelde, and the first vehicle rolled off the assembly line on July 17, 1965. During the next quarter-century, a total of 572,000 medium duty trucks were built at the plant.

The IFA W 50 was prominent among the transport trucks utilised by the North Vietnamese Army. Its early powerplant was the 108hp, four-cylinder KVD 14.5/12 diesel engine, generating a top speed of nearly 44mph and a range of 553 miles. Significant engine changes occurred in 1967 and 1973 to improve cold weather starting and other performance issues. The vehicle was more than 10ft high, over 22ft long and weighed almost six tons. It was capable of towing a load of nearly nine tons. ■

With East German markings, this IFA W 50 is shown with a large trailer in tow. *(Creative Commons LutzBruno via Wikimedia Commons)*

IFA W 50 conducting military operations in the Middle East in the 1980s. *(Government of Iran)*

A KrAZ-255 heavy truck crosses a bridge under construction. *(Creative Commons Олегъ via Wikimedia Commons)*

KrAZ-255

The Kremenchuk Automobile Plant (KrAZ) in Ukraine was founded in the wake of the Great Patriotic War on August 30, 1945, to produce farm equipment, bridging components and other machinery. In the spring of 1958, the Soviet Central Committee redirected its focus to that of heavy-duty truck manufacturing, transferring that function from the Yaroslavl Motor Plant (YaAZ). The first KrAZ vehicles were produced within the year.

One of the plant's contributions to the Soviet heavy truck inventory and to the North Vietnamese war effort was the flatbed 6X6 KrAZ-255, developed in the mid-1960s to replace the earlier KrAZ-214 that dated from the 1950s. The two types appeared quite similar, but the KrAZ-255 was provided with a more powerful engine and dependable transmission, new headlights and wider tyres to reduce ground pressure during offroad operations.

The KrAZ-255 entered production in 1967 and, during a run of 26 years, more than 160,000 were built, including several variants. The KrAZ-255 was the heaviest contemporary model at nearly 12 tons empty, while it stood nearly 10ft high, stretched more than 28ft long, and officially carried cargo of 7½ tons. Its 240hp V8 YaMZ-238 engine produced a top road speed of slightly more than 44mph with a range of 590 miles.

The KrAZ-255 was regularly used to tow heavy artillery pieces, including the 2A65, D-74 and M-46 howitzers, along with the T-12 anti-tank gun. It was also useful for towing aircraft. Variants included a command vehicle equipped with radio and communications gear and specialised radar. The vehicle and its chassis were also modified for engineering functions as a dump truck, logging truck, bridgelayer, military crane and excavator. In recent years, the Vietnamese government has sought to supplement and replace some of its self-propelled artillery vehicles, many

The heavy KrAZ-255 6X6 truck has demonstrated its versatility in military and civilian applications. *(Creative Commons Ralf Roletschek via Wikimedia Commons)*

of which are of US manufacture during the Vietnam War and were captured during the final communist offensive in the spring of 1975. One option involves the development of the PTH 130-K255B, mounting the Soviet-made M46 130mm field gun atop the chassis of the KrAZ-255. Some observers suggest that the Vietnamese vehicle is patterned after the Jupiter self-propelled gun developed in Cuba.

By the late 1970s, a supplemental vehicle designated the KrAZ-260 had entered production, with modifications to the cab design of the KrAZ-255 along with rearrangement of the interior spaces. The KrAZ-255 continued in production until 1994 when the new KrAZ-6322, an enhancement of the KrAZ-260, was approved for manufacture. ■

With canvas cargo cover in place, this KrAZ-255 was in service with the Russian Air Force in 2011. *(Creative Commons Vitaly V. Kuzmin via Wikimedia Commons)*

MAZ-502

The four-wheel-drive MAZ-502 was a derivative of the MAZ-200 truck family. *(Creative Commons Igor via Wikimedia Commons)*

During World War Two, the Soviet Red Army relied on US-made all-wheel-drive trucks obtained via the Lend-Lease programme for the majority of its cross-country transport. Most Soviet truck types had been manufactured prior to the war and were outdated, with the development of Russian all-wheel-drive vehicles lagging behind.

In 1947, the first Soviet-manufactured truck with a diesel engine, the 4X2 MAZ-200, went into production at the Yaroslavl Automobile Plant northeast of Moscow. By 1950, production of the MAZ-200 was moved to the Minsk Automobile Plant (MAZ) in Belarus, where assembly continued through 1965. During the period, numerous improvements and upgrades were made to the basic MAZ-200, while MAZ-205 dump truck, MAZ-501 logging truck and MAZ-200V tractor trailer variants were also produced.

Along with the development of the MAZ-501 logging truck, an all-wheel-drive military truck became a priority, which led to the production of the MAZ-502, a general purpose 4X4 that was the first vehicle specifically produced for the military at the Minsk facility. Production of the MAZ-502 continued until the end of the MAZ-200 run, and while relatively few were in operation with the Red Army, the vehicle was also exported to the German Democratic Republic and North Vietnam during the 1960s.

The 4X4 MAZ-502 weighed 3.85 tons empty and carried a maximum payload of 4.4 tons. It stood nearly 9ft high, stretched to a length of more than 23ft and was almost 9ft wide, while the cabin provided space for a driver and two others. The original production flatbed vehicle was tested with an enclosure combining steel and wood, but eventually it was decided that the area would essentially become a steel box that could accommodate cargo or troops, with a canvas tarpaulin for cover. The 135hp, four-cylinder YaAZ-M204V diesel engine, a holdover from the earliest production days at the Yaroslavl facility, produced a top speed of 31mph. In the last year of production, a series of tests including water injection were conducted with the intention of improving engine performance, but these all failed to meet expectations and were terminated.

From 1961, towing capability was added to the MAZ-502 for the transport of artillery, missile systems and trailer-borne cargo. Some flatbed MAZ-502 vehicles were also equipped with a forward winch for vehicle recovery and later civilian use in forestry as the M-502A, while the M-502B was a tractor variant paired with rolling stock trailers to transport freight.

Today, examples of the MAZ-502 are quite rare, surviving primarily as museum pieces. It is believed that a number of them were destroyed or abandoned during the Chernobyl nuclear plant disaster in 1986. ∎

The cargo area of the MAZ-502 was accessed through a hinged tailgate. *(Creative Commons Igor via Wikimedia Commons)*

The MAZ-502 interior was basic, with utilitarian steering and gauges. *(Creative Commons Igor via Wikimedia Commons)*

UralZIS-355M

UralZIS-355M topping an outdoor monument to the Russian armed forces. *(Creative Commons Дмитрий Костоусов via Wikimedia Commons)*

The Nazi invasion of the Soviet Union on June 22, 1941, known as Operation Barbarossa, was highly successful in its early stages and threatened to overrun industrial centres that were critical to the Soviet economy and its future war effort. In response to the German onslaught, the Stalin Automotive Plant (ZIS) was relocated in the autumn of 1941 from the Moscow area to the relative safety of Ulyanovsk on the River Volga and Miass in the Chelyabinsk Oblast in the Ural Mountains on the natural border between Eastern Europe and Asia.

On July 8, 1944, the first complete ZIS-5 4X2 truck was produced at the Miass facility and, when the war ended, assembly continued under the brand name UralZIS. The truck had proven itself reliable and rugged during World War Two, particularly during the horrific 900-day siege of t Leningrad, transporting badly needed supplies to the civilian population amid difficult weather conditions and under enemy fire.

In the post-war years, improvements to the ZIS-5 continued. In 1946, a new variant was introduced as the 2½-ton ZIS-352, followed in 1956 by the UralZIS-355, a change that had virtually nothing to do with design improvements but was done largely to match Soviet sequential numbering. Two years later, this designation was changed to UralZIS-355M

This gleaming UralZIS-355M is today a museum piece in Russia. *(Creative Commons Sergey Korovkin 84 via Wikimedia Commons)*

with the 'M" standing for 'Modernised'. During the period of de-Stalinisation that occurred in the late 1950s, the truck was renamed the Ural-355M, but remains widely known today by its earlier UralZIS moniker.

Rooted in the successful ZIS-5, the UralZIS-355M was built until 1965, with noteworthy improvements undertaken from late 1957. The medium duty vehicle was powered by a 95hp, six-cylinder petrol engine generating a top speed of 43mph and weighed 3.7 tons empty. Its maximum payload was in excess of 3¾ tons, while the vehicle stood nearly 7ft tall with a length of almost 21ft. The UralZIS-355M was the last dedicated medium duty truck produced at the Ural facility. By the late

1960s, assembly had transitioned to vehicles that focused on offroad performance.

From the 1930s to the 1960s, when the ZIS-5 series was produced in the Soviet Union, more than a million examples are believed to have been completed. Many of these were exported to Soviet client states, including North Vietnam, where they transported supplies and ammunition along the Ho Chi Minh Trail, the famed infiltration route from the north through Laos and Cambodia to South Vietnam during the Vietnam conflict.

Remarkably, only a few examples of the UralZIS-355M remain today, several of them as museum pieces in Russia. ■

This UralZIS-355M hauls a light trailer in its museum display. Note the dual rear wheels. *(Creative Commons Sergey Korovkin 84 via Wikimedia Commons)*

ZIL-130

The embossed grille of the ZIL-130 is prominent in this Ukrainian vehicle. *(Creative Commons VargaA via Wikimedia Commons)*

ZIL-130 packed with soldiers of the North Korean Army during a parade in Pyongyang. *(Creative Commons Uwe Brodrecht via Wikimedia Commons)*

By the late 1950s, Josef Stalin, the despotic premier who had led the country for decades and through the Great Patriotic War, had fallen into disfavour following his death in 1953. His name was erased from many aspects of collective consciousness, including the ZIS Stalin Auto Plant in the Moscow area, which from 1956 was known as ZIL for 'Likhachev'.

Manufacturing of vehicles in the Soviet Union did not change in name only. Government leaders recognised the need to modernise their long-serving ZIS-150 general purpose truck, which had been prominent during the 1950s as a military transport. The ZIS-150 was derived from the 1930s ZIS-5. Its immediate successor, the ZIL-164, was only an upgrade of the existing ZIS-150 and was not considered a lasting solution to the growing needs of the modern Red Army.

With the end of de-Stalinisation, engineers at the ZIL auto facility began work on a true successor to the ZIS-150. The resulting 4X2 ZIL-130 was destined to become a significant transport vehicle in the Soviet Union and among satellite states for well over 50 years. The production run of the ZIL-130 including prototypes ran from 1962 to 2012 and the design was adapted, updated and modified on numerous occasions. Assembly facilities at Chita and Novouralsk also built the truck and more than 3½ million are believed to have been completed.

The design of the ZIL-130 was a departure in terms of mechanics and style. The cabin was completely redone, including a wider windshield that wrapped further around both sides to provide an improved field of vision for the driver. Power steering was introduced, along with an upgraded transmission, while Erik Sabo, a young graduate of the Moscow School of Art and Industry, was enlisted to provide an overall aesthetic that included an embossed radiator grille, more pleasing lines and contours and attention to the comfort of the operators - elements that had previously seldom been seen in Soviet vehicle design.

The new ZIL-130 was several years in development and mass production did not begin until October 1964. An early six-cylinder powerplant was found inadequate and was replaced by a robust 150hp V8 engine that produced a top speed of 56mph. The vehicle weighed 4¾ tons, carried a payload of 6.86 tons, stood nearly 8ft high and was almost 22ft long. Numerous variants were built through the years, including the 6X4 ZIL-133 and the 6X6 ZIL-131.

The longevity of the ZIL-130 is testament to its durability and contribution to commercial and military activities in the Soviet Union. The vehicle was sent to North Vietnam in substantial numbers during the war and was known to have participated with Vietnamese forces in the border conflict with the People's Republic of China in the late 1970s. ∎

A ZIL-130 preserved as a monument in Russia. *(Creative Commons MarSaf via Wikimedia Commons)*

ZIL-151

ZIL-151 trucks towing artillery pieces and a complement of Red Army soldiers during a parade.
(Creative Commons Nagy Gyula via Wikimedia Commons)

The first post-World War Two medium duty truck produced in the Soviet Union, the ZIL-151 was an evolution of the preceding Soviet-built ZIS-6 and the US-made Studebaker US6. The American truck was one of numerous vehicles the Soviets had received during the wartime Lend-Lease programme, and while Soviet engineers had been adept at developing new tanks and self-propelled armoured vehicles, the same could not be said of the standard trucks that were necessary to ensure troop movement and hauling of supplies.

When the Soviets received American trucks they were impressed with their offroad capabilities. Earlier Soviet designs had been intended for use primarily on improved roads and had struggled in difficult terrain. Stalin Automotive Factory No 2 took the lead in the development of a more robust Soviet medium duty truck in the waning days of the war and the two-axle prototype ZIS-150P, similar to the ZIS-150, was completed in 1944. However, initial testing revealed the vehicle was too heavy, so a three-axle design was adopted in late 1945. Two prototypes were completed the following year, one with dual rear wheels and the other with single rear wheels.

Tests in the summer of 1947 produced favourable results and the dual-wheeled ZIS-151 entered full production in April 1948, although delays were experienced due to the US ending shipments of tooling equipment.

Meanwhile, the Stalin factory received a directive for the production of an armoured personnel carrier based on the ZIS-151 chassis. Initially called Object 140, this project went on to become the well-known BTR-152. Another initiative based on the ZIS-151 chassis led to the production of the ZIS-485 (BAV-485) amphibious vehicle. In 1956, the Soviet de-Stalinisation programme brought a change in the original factory name to Zavod Imeni Likhacheva and the permanent designation of the vehicle became ZIL-151.

The ZIL-151 was found to perform below expectations in mud or swampland, with the dual wheel arrangement at least partially to blame. This issue was addressed in the follow-on ZIL-157, which had single rear wheels. However, from 1948-1958, the 6X6 ZIL-151 was the production general purpose truck of the Soviet military and approximately 150,000 were built. The vehicle was powered by a 92hp, six-cylinder petrol engine that produced a maximum speed of 37mph on improved roads with a range of more than 300 miles. The ZIL-151 weighed slightly more than six tons, stood more than 7½ft high and was almost 23ft long, with a payload of two tons.

The ZIL-151 was a solid platform to carry the 'Katyusha' mobile rocket launch systems for which the Red Army had become famous during World War Two. It was further produced in bridgelaying, firefighting, tractor-trailer and other variants, some including upgraded components. An export version was offered to Soviet client states, including North Vietnam, while a copy of the ZIL-151 called the Jiefang CA-30 was built in the People's Republic of China from 1956. The improved CA-30 equivalent of the ZIL-157 remained in production through the mid-1980s. ∎

This ZIL-151 mounts a BM-13-16 'Katyusha' rocket launcher. *(Creative Commons Taco Witte via Wikimedia Commons)*

ZIL-151 truck in a museum in Verkhnyaya Pyshma, Sverdlovskaya Oblast, Russia, with an artillery piece in tow. *(Creative Commons Mir76-ghost via Wikimedia Commons)*

ZIL-157/157K

ZIL-157 towing a ZU-23-2 57mm anti-aircraft gun at an air base in Israel. *(Creative Commons Bukvoed via Wikimedia Commons)*

The Ho Chi Minh Trail, the infamous infiltration and supply route from North Vietnam to communist forces in the south during the Vietnam war, was a labyrinth of improved roads, dirt tracks, waterways and jungle terrain that stretched nearly 10,000 miles. During the course of US involvement in the conflict, air and ground offensives to sever the trail proved frustrating. Transport was accomplished on foot, by boat, via pack animal and, whenever possible, by truck.

The Central Intelligence Agency reported in February 1972 that between 1965 and 1971 the North Vietnamese had lost an estimated 47,600 trucks due to interdiction. But the tenacity of the supply endeavour is a testament not only to the resolve and resilience of the people involved but also the rugged performance of their medium duty trucks.

Particularly significant in the supply line were trucks of the ZIL-151 series, which entered production in 1948 as the first post-World War Two vehicles of their kind built in the Soviet Union and were exported to North Vietnam as military aid. The ZIL-151s were a familiar sight during the war and their elongated hoods and radiator grilles gave rise to the nickname 'Crocodile'. Further development of the ZIL-151 followed in the 1950s and the emergence of the improved vehicles stretched the production run of the series into the 1990s and easily topped one million vehicles.

The vast majority of these – nearly 800,000 – were the ZIL-157 model that was manufactured at various intervals from 1958 to 1994. Early improved trucks were known as the ZIS-157 due to production at the Josef Stalin automotive plant in Moscow. This designation was changed

This ZIL-157 medium duty truck has been outfitted as a command and control vehicle. *(Creative Commons Max Bubnovsky via Wikimedia Commons)*

along with that of other vehicles to ZIL, erasing the former dictator's name during the de-Staliniszation programme undertaken in the mid-1950s. This identified the manufacturer as the Likhachev plant, although the ZIL-157 was also built at the Ural (UAmZ) facility in Amur Oblast in the 1970s. In time, ZIL-157s were also license-built in the People's Republic of China as the Jiefang CA-30, which was also supplied to North Vietnam in great numbers.

Although the 6X6 ZIL-151 was the standard medium duty general purpose truck of the Red Army from 1948 to approximately 1958, a programme to improve its performance was underway shortly after the truck was authorised for mass production. Its operation in offroad conditions had been disappointing, so steps were taken to address this shortcoming. Still, the vehicle lacked power steering and, at times, the driver was

required to exhibit significant physical strength just to handle the truck in difficult terrain.

The original ZIL-157 powerplant was a 104hp, six-cylinder diesel engine producing a top speed of just over 40mph. The vehicle weighed 2½ tons and stood 9ft high with a length of nearly 23ft and width of 7.7ft. Its maximum cross-country payload was 3.3 tons, which increased to more than eight tons with a trailer in tow on improved roads.

While there were few changes to its outward appearance and the cabin was virtually the same in both the ZIL-151 and ZIL-157, the latter introduced larger single tyres on the rear axles rather than the smaller tyres on the earlier configuration. This step was taken to improve cross country performance, but the most significant enhancement to that aspect of the

A searchlight has been mounted in the cargo area of this ZIL-157 on display in Minsk, Belarus. *(Creative Commons Homoatrox via Wikimedia Commons)*

vehicle's varied missions was the installation of an adjustable tyre pressure system that allowed air pressure in the individual tyres to be increased or decreased according to the terrain, improving traction substantially in snow, ice, mud and swampland. A particularly beneficial aspect of the system was its ability to reinflate a tyre and maintain some pressure even after a puncture. One notable creature comfort was the introduction of a cabin heater, which was a welcome addition during winter operations.

Testing and evaluation had been conducted sometime between 1954 and 1957, with mass production of the ZIL-157 beginning in 1958. In the field, the new version of the 6X6 truck exhibited good characteristics. By1961, the further improved ZIL-157K incorporated an automatic tyre pressure adjusting control and was equipped with a more powerful 109hp, six-cylinder petrol engine delivering an equivalent top speed of just over 40mph.

The ZIL-157K was manufactured in Moscow until 1978, when the line was transferred to the UAmZ truck assembly plant in eastern Russia. The UAmZ version of the truck, dubbed the ZIL-157KD, increased the onboard payload to five tons on improved roads and three tons cross country. This variant was built until 1992 and remaining components were expended from stockpiles to conclude manufacturing two years later. The ZIL-157V, a tractor trailer version, was also available from 1961 and was upgraded to the ZIL-157KDV variant in 1978, and employed in civilian as well as military applications.

Aside from the Soviet Union, the People's Republic of China and North Vietnam, other major users of the ZIL-151 and ZIL-157 medium duty trucks included North Korea, Syria, Egypt, Albania, Ukraine, Finland, Indonesia and Iraq. ■

A ZIL-157V tractor towing a Volkhov 6009 anti-aircraft missile package. (Creative Commons AlfvanBeem via Wikimedia Commons)

ZIL-157 mounting a Czech-built 130mm rocket launcher system. (Creative Commons Tourbillon via Wikimedia Commons)

Chinese-built CA-30s participating in a Victory Day parade in North Korea. *(Creative Commons Stefan Krasowski via Wikimedia Commons)*

CA-30

The Soviet Union was the primary benefactor of the People's Republic of China after the communist armed forces of Mao Tse-Tung emerged victorious from their long civil war. The foreign aid extended by the Soviets was both civilian and military in nature, with the two countries signing the Treaty of Friendship, Alliance and Mutual Assistance on February 14, 1950.

By 1956, with Soviet assistance, the Chinese had built their Batou Tank Plant, officially named the Inner Mongolia Factory 617, to produce the Type 59, a copy of the Soviet T-54. On July 13 of the same year, the First Automotive Works (FAW) was established at Changchun, Jilin Province, to produce the CA-10, a copy of the Soviet 4X2 ZIL-150. Soon after, FAW began building the CA-30, a copy of the ZIL-151 and its improved model, the ZIL-157. In turn, each of the trucks involved in CA-10 and CA-30 development and production traced its lineage in some form to the US trucks provided to the Soviet Union through Lend-Lease during World War Two or license-built prior to the war.

Production of the CA-30 began in 1958 and continued into the late 1970s or mid-1980s, according to different sources. The truck was made available for commercial use, although its military application was readily apparent and it was procured in substantial quantities by the Chinese government. The 6X6 CA-30 assembly was facilitated by the use of some common components from the CA-10. It weighed 5.89 tons empty and carried a payload of nearly five tons on improved roads and 2¾ tons cross country. It stood 7¾ft high, stretched almost 22ft, and was roughly 7½ft wide.

The truck was rugged and dependable, serving widely with the Chinese People's Liberation Army, while thousands of examples were shipped to North Vietnam for use by its regular army and the Viet Cong insurgency. With its heavy capacity, the CA-30 became a workhorse of the Chinese and North Vietnamese armed forces, and many remained in service into the 1990s.

CA-30 modified as a 'Katyusha' rocket launch platform. *(Creative Commons Gary Todd via Wikimedia Commons)*

The CA-30 powerplant was the 95hp, six-cylinder Jiefang 120 petrol engine generating a top road speed of 40mph. In similar fashion to the ZIL-157, the CA-10 was a large flatbed that facilitated several modifications for specialised uses, including a dump truck, tractor/freight hauler, tanker, rocket launch platform, radar and command centre and troop transport.

One prominent distinguishing feature between the CA-30 and the ZIL-157 was the fenders. Early Chinese trucks sported rounded fenders like the Soviet version, but the CA-30 had squared fenders for the majority of its manufacturing life. ■

CA-30 command and radar truck on display at a museum in the People's Republic of China. *(Creative Commons BrokenSphere via Wikimedia Commons)*

An abandoned AT-L light artillery tractor. *(Creative Commons Aleksandr Markin via Wikimedia Commons)*

AT-L

The AT-L light artillery tractor was an early Cold War-era vehicle designed primarily to haul the 160mm field artillery pieces of the Red Army. Its replacement, the AT-LM, was also being developed for the heavier 240mm gun at the same time. When the AT-L was found inadequate in some respects, it was eventually retired in favour of the AT-LM. However, at least a few of those remaining in service found their way to Southeast Asia and were utilised by the North Vietnamese Army during the Vietnam conflict.

The engineering effort that produced the AT-L was undertaken at the Kharkov Tractor Plant's design bureau in 1947. The vehicle incorporated a tank chassis paired with the cab of a ZIS-150 or ZIL-164 truck and the front grille of a GAZ-51. Three prototypes underwent extensive testing in 1947-1948 and modifications were made before the AT-L was accepted by the Red Army in 1949, entering production the following year and reaching frontline military units in 1953. It was produced at the Kharkov facility until 1967 and was used to tow various field guns, howitzers and mortars, being required to be able to traverse a field trench of at least 3¼ft.

Its original welded, box-shaped hull was intended to provide enhanced cross country capability and to lighten the vehicle. However, it was discarded because vibrations shook the thin sheet steel severely at higher speed. The original chassis was also improved in the mid-1950s and resulted in a variant designated the ATL-5A.

The AT-L was relatively light at about nine tons with a load capacity of two tons. It stood nearly 7¼ft tall, was 17½ft long and its flatbed was enclosed by folding panels. The cabin could accommodate three crewmen if necessary, but essentially provided a seat for the driver and a sleeping bunk. It was accessed by conventional doors on either side. The vehicle could also serve as a troop transport if required, with folding accommodations for eight soldiers. The AT-L was capable of towing trailers or weapons systems weighing up to six tons.

The 135hp, four-cylinder diesel engine provided a top speed of 26mph and the vehicle's typical range while towing was about 186 miles. In 1962, the AT-LM was introduced with two additional 130-litre fuel tanks to extend its range. A number of AT-Ls were equipped as command vehicles, fitted with the SNAR-1, SNAR-2 and ARSO-2 artillery radar reconnaissance systems. Other variants included a bridgelayer, firefighting vehicle and some models capable of accommodating bulldozer equipment.

Other military operators included the People's Republic of China, Syria, Bulgaria, Hungary, Poland and North Korea. Although largely relegated to reserve status or retired from Red Army in the 1960s, the AT-L was commercially viable with industry for years afterward and some remained in service through the 1990s. ■

AT-L light artillery tractor on display at the Yad la-Shiryon Museum in Israel. *(Creative Commons Bukvoed via Wikimedia Commons)*

An AT-LM gun tractor negotiates a slope during a review of military vehicles. *(Creative Commons Alf van Beem via Wikimedia Commons)*

AT-S / ATS-59

The AT-S prime mover carried up to 16 crewmen to service an artillery piece in tow. *(Creative Commons Tourbillon via Wikimedia Commons)*

An ATS-59 medium artillery prime mover in desert colours displayed in a museum in **Israel.** *(Creative Commons Bukvoed via Wikimedia Commons)*

After World War Two, the Soviet Union continued to produce artillery tractors to equip the Red Army in anticipation of a war with Western powers and the subsequent NATO alliance. The Soviet high command expected the military confrontation to take place on the relatively flat plains of Eastern and Central Europe. Instead, East and West did not collide directly, but engaged in a number of proxy wars around the globe.

Soviet economic and military aid stretched from its European satellite states to the African continent and Southeast Asia, where the communist government of North Vietnam was a willing recipient of military hardware, including heavy machinery such as the AT-S and ATS-59 artillery movers. Development of the AT-S (Artilleriyskiy Tyagach – Sredniy or Artillery Tractor – Medium) was undertaken in 1950 and, two years later, serial production began at the Chelyabinsk Tractor Plant (ChTZ) in the Ural Mountains. In 1955, production began at the Kurgan Machine Building Plant (KMZ) in the southern Urals.

The AT-S was capable of transporting a total of 16 troops to operate the vehicle and service the artillery piece in tow. Its seating forward included space for the driver and six others, while the rear cargo area was open and could be covered with a canvas tarpaulin. The AT-S weighed 12 tons empty and was capable of transporting three tons of cargo or seating 10 soldiers. The vehicle stood just over 8ft to the cab roof, stretched 19¼ft long and nearly 8½ft wide. Powered by the 275hp V-12 V-54-T diesel engine, it was capable of a top road speed of nearly 22mph with a range of 182 miles. Its production run ended after a decade.

The smaller AT-L prime mover also entered service in 1952, after research and testing dating back to 1947. Production was initiated in 1950 at the Kharkov Tractor Plant (KhTZ) in Ukraine and its manufacturing extended well beyond that of the AT-S into the mid-1960s.

By 1959, the Soviets were seeking a replacement for the AT-S, with the improved ATS-59 entering production at Kurgan in the early 1960s. The new model incorporated a more robust 300hp V-12 diesel engine which produced a top speed of just over 24mph and a range of nearly 218 miles. The development of the ATS-59 was accompanied by an effort to standardise Soviet Bloc artillery tractors, which limited the production of the contemporary Polish Mazur D-350.

The follow-on ATS-59G utilised the same 520hp, 12-cylinder V-55 diesel engine as the T-55 main battle tank and was upgraded to include protection against nuclear, biological and chemical weapons (NBC).

In 2023, a Russian ATS-59G mounting a 25mm 2M-3M naval gun was observed operating against Ukrainian forces. ∎

The ATS-59G artillery tractor was powered by the same engine as the T-55 main battle tank. *(Creative Commons Marko M via Wikimedia Commons)*

MAZUR D-350

A Polish soldier by a Mazur D-350 with canvas tarpaulin in place. *(Grzes1966 Public Domain)*

Although manufactured in a relatively small quantity, the Mazur D-350 prime mover did find its way into wartime service. Design work began in 1956 at the Josef Stalin Mechanical Factory in the city of Labedy in Silesia, Poland, and only about 1,000 examples were completed between 1958 and 1960. Of these, 218 were sold to Czechoslovakia, while 50 are known to have been sent to North Vietnam for service during the Vietnam war. The balance of the vehicles went into service with the Polish People's Army and remained active until the 1970s.

By the late 1950s, Poland was building the Soviet-designed T-54 tank under license, with the effort to develop an artillery tractor based on the tank's chassis getting underway in 1957. During that year, two prototypes designated ACS Mazur D-300 were completed and, in 1958, two more were finished using roughly 75% of the components of the T-54. After a short test and evaluation period, the Mazur-350 entered production.

Three facilities were involved in the construction of the Mazur D-350. While the body, drivetrain and wheels were built at Labedy, a defence contractor founded in southeastern Poland in the late 1930s, Huta Stalowa Wowa, manufactured the suspension and chassis, while the engine was produced at PZL Wola, a relatively new supplier that had been founded in Warsaw in 1951.

The Mazur D-350 proved itself adept at its primary task and was particularly noted for towing the M30 122mm howitzer in cross country exercises. The prime mover earned the nickname of 'Gomulkova's Revenge' probably in honour of

The Polish Mazur D-350 was overshadowed by the Soviet-built ATS-59 prime mover. *(Wisnia6522 Public Domain)*

Wladislaw Gomulkova, who was the foremost leader of post-war Poland from 1947 to 1948 and again from 1956 to 1970. At times, Gomulkova fell out of favour with the Soviet government, choosing a course at odds with the prevailing influence of Moscow. Despite its fine field characteristics, the Mazur D-350 production run was short, due to the Soviet preference for its own ATS-59 artillery prime mover and the effort to standardise equipment among Eastern Bloc countries.

The Mazur D-350 was typically operated by a driver and mechanic, while its rear compartment could accommodate a crew of eight to service the gun in tow. The vehicle weighed nearly 15 tons loaded for combat, with a cargo capacity of approximately 13¾ tons and capable of towing a trailer or artillery piece at just over 27½ tons. Its 350hp, 12-cylinder W-54 diesel engine produced a top road speed of 33mph, with a fully loaded range of 305 miles. The vehicle stood nearly 9ft high and was 19ft long with a width of 9½ft. Vehicles that were deactivated from military service sometimes found new applications in forestry and the railroad industry. ■

Mazur D-350 with a 122mm M30 howitzer in tow. *(Wisnia6522 Public Domain)*

CA-10

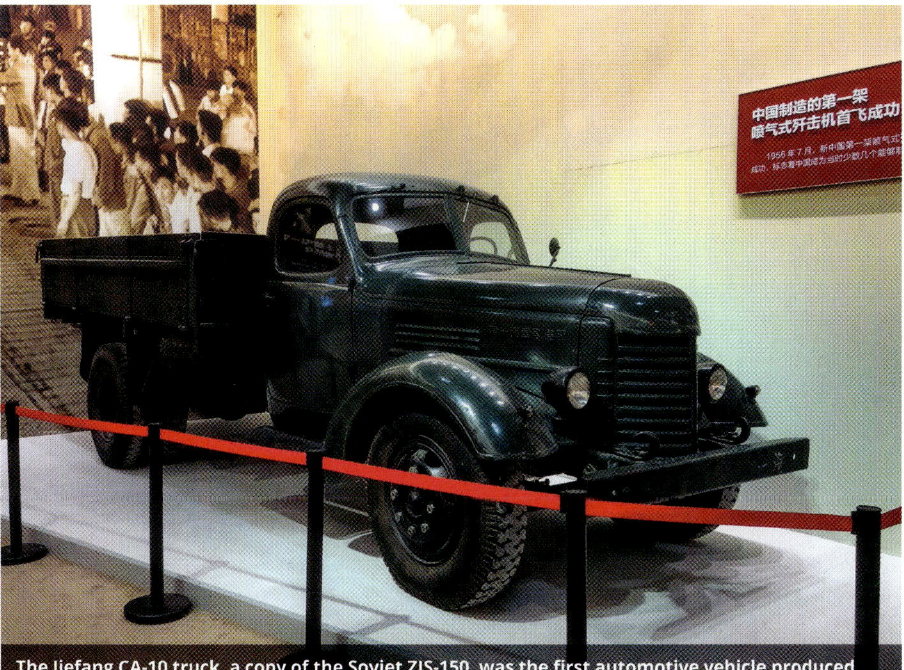

The Jiefang CA-10 truck, a copy of the Soviet ZIS-150, was the first automotive vehicle produced under the Chinese communist regime. *(Creative Commons N509FZ via Wikimedia Commons)*

Chinese workers at FAW celebrate their production of the CA-10. *(Creative Commons 袁苓 via Wikimedia Commons)*

The People's Republic of China was established in 1949 and the new government signed the Treaty of Friendship, Alliance and Mutual Assistance with the Soviet Union on February 14, 1950. During the decade that followed, the Soviets supplied aid in many forms to the new Chinese regime, including military equipment such as vehicles built by the Soviets themselves and US-built surplus received through Lend-Lease during World War Two. Among these were examples of the ZIS-150 truck, which entered production in 1947 and borrowed much of its design from the Studebaker US6 2½-ton truck and the K7 built by International Harvester.

With Soviet assistance, the Chinese opened the Inner Mongolia Factory 617, otherwise known as the Batou Tank Plant, in 1956 to produce the Type 59 version of the T-54 tank. At the same time, work began on a facility dubbed the First Automotive Works (FAW) at Changchun in Jilin Province, tasked with producing the Jiefang CA-10, a Chinese copy of the ZIS-150.

The first 4X2 CA-10 was completed at FAW on July 13, 1956, becoming not only the first truck produced in the People's Republic of China, but the first automotive product of any kind successfully manufactured by the communist government.

The CA-10 was produced into the 1980s in China, with numbers exceeding one million, and the vehicle became an icon in the vast nation. Other countries also built the truck during its 30-year run, with total production believed to have topped two million.

The relatively short flatbed CA-10 was widely exported to communist countries, including North Vietnam, then embroiled in its long war against the US-supported South Vietnamese military. The CA-10 became a common sight on the famous Ho Chi Minh Trail, the long supply and infiltration line through which men, machines, and munitions passed to the Viet Cong insurgency. Although its performance in difficult terrain was not great, the 4X2 CA-10 became a regular workhorse.

The truck was powered by a 90hp, six-cylinder petrol engine virtually identical to that of the ZIS-150, producing a top speed just over 40mph. It weighed just under four tons, with a height of more than 7ft and a length of about 20ft. It carried a maximum payload of four tons and was also used as a prime mover for light artillery. The 6X6 CA-30 variant entered production in 1964. ■

The Jiefang CA-10 bears a resemblance to several influential trucks of the 1940s. *(Creative Commons N509FZ via Wikimedia Commons)*

ZIS-150

he US Central Intelligence Agency released a report on December 3, 1951, describing the characteristics of the Soviet Union's ZIS-150 truck in detail. The influence of American auto manufacturers, including Ford, Studebaker, International Harvester and others, was no doubt apparent to the CIA analysts. The report was marked top secret and remained classified for 60 years until the autumn of 2011. It read: "The Moscow Automotive Plant Stalin has begun the series production of the ZIS-150 truck, a four-wheel machine with rear wheel drive (4x2). The ZIS-150 is designed to carry loads up to 4 tons on hard-topped roads, but, over rough terrain, the speed of the truck and the load carried must be reduced… The small amount of operating experience acquired to date has proved the good quality and reliability of the ZIS-150 truck."

The development of the ZIS-150 dates back to the mid-1930s, when the Soviets sought a replacement for their outmoded ZIS-5 truck and their experience building the Ford AA light truck under license had spurred new engineering efforts. The ZIS-15 prototype was ready by 1938, but world events took centre stage. The Great Patriotic War interrupted further development until 1944, when more Western technology was available and the course of the conflict had turned in favour of the Allies.

Subsequent tests revealed that the vehicle's original 82hp engine was insufficient, which was rectified with the introduction of a 95hp, six-cylinder petrol engine that delivered a top speed of over 40mph and range of slightly more than 260 miles. The ZIS-150 weighed just over 4¼ tons, stood just over 7ft high and slightly more than 22ft long.

Production began on April 27, 1948, and the vehicle was manufactured in the Soviet Union, Romania, Georgia and China into the mid-1980s, with slight variations. The most notable of these was the Chinese CA-10 series.

During the 1950s the ZIS-150 and the GAZ-51 had served as the primary Red Army trucks. In 1956, the Soviet programme of de-Stalinisation resulted in a name change at the Moscow plant, after which the ZIS-150 was referred to as the ZIL-150.

Two quite similar models, the ZIL-164 and ZIL-166, entered production in 1957, with total production of the ZIS-150 family topping two million. North Vietnam received a large number of the Chinese CA-10 variant, while the Soviet Union, the largest supplier of rolling stock to North Vietnam during the Vietnam war, also sent the ZIS-150 in quantity. ∎

Farm workers loading harvested wheat on a ZIS-150 for transport. *(Creative Commons Bundesarchiv Bild via Wikimedia Commons)*

A crane loads building materials into the flatbed of a ZIS-150. *(Creative Commons Deutsche Fotothek via Wikimedia Commons)*

The Soviet ZIS-150 truck incorporated features gleaned from US models built under license and received through Lend-Lease. *(Creative Commons Jeka3000 via Wikimedia Commons)*

ZIS-485

This post-Vietnam War example of the ZIS-485 has been converted for civilian use. *(Creative Commons Daidien via Wikimedia Commons)*

In the Red Army, the ZIS-485 was known more officially as the BAV-485, the acronym for Bolshoi Avtomobil Vodoplavayushchiy or 'Big Car Waterfowl'. It was an accurate description as the ZIS-485 was a Soviet-built copy of the famous American DUKW 6X6 amphibious vehicle obtained from the United States via Lend-Lease during World War Two. The Soviets received nearly 600 examples of the DUKW and found its remarkable toughness, hauling capacity and ability to negotiate rivers, streams, swamps, beaches and muddy tracks appealing.

As their fast-moving tactics evolved across Eastern Europe during the latter year of the Great Patriotic War, the Soviets prized the aptitude of amphibious vehicles and intended the ZIS-485 to serve alongside the GAZ-46 4X4 wheeled amphibious reconnaissance vehicle that had also entered service in the 1950s.

The prototype ZIS-485 was built in 1949 at the Josef Stalin Automobile Plant (ZIS) at Dnepropetrovsk (DAZ) as Project 485 under the direction of chief designer VA Grachev. Actual manufacturing was transferred to the primary ZIS facility and the first production model was completed in 1952. Thereafter, annual output totalled nearly 500 vehicles for the next decade at various industrial locations in the Soviet Union, including the First State Josef Stalin Automobile Plant, the Bryansk Automobile Plant and the Dnepropetrovsk Automobile Plant.

The ZIS-485 utilised the chassis of the ZIS-151 6X6 truck with a boat-like hull of rather thin welded steel that offered little protection against even small-arms fire. Its 110hp, six-cylinder ZiS123 petrol engine was mounted at the front to produce a top speed of 37mph and a range of 329 miles on land or 6mph in water with a dedicated propeller system engaged. The vehicle stood nearly 9ft high, was just over 31ft long and weighed more than 10½ tons. A rear door facilitated passenger boarding or loading cargo. The passenger/cargo area was open-topped, but could be covered by a canvas tarpaulin.

The ZIS-485 was a Soviet copy of the US amphibious DUKW vehicle of World War Two. *(Wisnia 6522 Public Domain)*

Red Army soldiers with their amphibious ZIS-485, also known as the BAV-485. *(Creative Commons Олегъ via Wikimedia Commons)*

The ZIS-485 was usually operated by two crew members, with the driver behind a wide windscreen split into two sections. The vehicle was typically unarmed, but in some cases a 12.7mm heavy machine gun was installed for anti-aircraft defence. The ZIS-485 was widely used by the Red Army, the Polish Army of the Warsaw Pact and in Vietnam until the late 1970s, when newer types of vehicles offered extensive modernisation, such as protection against nuclear, biological and chemical weapons. Upgrades through the years included a transition to the chassis of the ZIL-157 truck, which was designated the ZIS-485A. ∎

VIETNAM VEHICLES IN VIEW

South Vietnamese and Australian soldiers atop an M113 during Operation Phoi Hop, 1971. *(Creative Commons Cunneen, William James Australian War Memorial)*

US soldiers and Bell UH-1 'Huey' helicopters working together in Vietnam in 1971. *(National Archives and Records Administration)*

The 'Hueys' brought men into battle from above and the airmobile tactic – once theory – was put into practice. Though tank vs tank encounters were few, they were nevertheless savage.

Even convoy duty evolved into a dangerous game of cat and mouse. Learning quickly to respect the stealth of the Viet Cong guerrillas they faced along roads and trails through South Vietnam, inventive Americans installed machine guns aboard some of the supply vehicles and turned them into 'gun trucks' to provide some measure of defence.

Through the course of the conflict, vehicles demonstrated aptitude for the job at hand. They were also found to be inadequate at times, failing to perform as intended. They were upgunned, jury-rigged, patched and repurposed, scrapped, blasted, burned and crashed. And they influenced the outcome of the conflict in an immeasurable way. Many survive today as museum pieces, monuments and memorials. Still others lie where they were disabled and abandoned, rusting and gradually being engulfed by jungle vines and vegetation.

This volume has offered a glimpse of the machines that men utilised in victory and defeat during one of the longest and most gruelling armed conflicts in military history. ∎

The crucial role played by mechanisation during the Vietnam conflict cannot be understated. Tanks, trucks, self-propelled artillery, armoured personnel carriers, Jeeps, helicopters and more were deployed to deliver troops, materiel and decisive fire in critical situations. The vehicles that participated bridge the advancing technology from the mid-20th Century to the present day, some of them fielded to fight a war in Central and Eastern Europe only to be sent into action amid the rice paddies, plains, jungles and mountains of Vietnam.

An old story survives from the Viet Minh victory over the French at Dien Bien Phu in the spring of 1954. The French had fortified their positions in a bowl-shaped valley and Viet Minh General Vo Nguyen Giap realized that his forces could rain artillery fire down on the Europeans from the surrounding heights. The only problem, seemingly insurmountable, was getting the artillery pieces up the steep mountainsides. No motorised transport could accomplish the task. So Giap's dedicated soldiers manhandled the artillery up the slopes. It was dangerous work and one man actually threw himself in front of a gun that had gotten away from its handlers and begun to roll backward down a mountain. He gave his life for the nationalist/communist cause.

With the introduction of the helicopter, American and South Vietnamese soldiers quite regularly transported critical supplies to besieged bases or outposts deep in the Central Highlands of the country, along with heavier weapons such as tanks and artillery. These pilots and aircrew demonstrated equal dedication, accomplishing their missions at great hazard.

A Soviet-built PT-76 light tank and other vehicles of the conflict at the Army Museum in the Vietnamese capital of Hanoi. *(Creative Commons calflier001 via Wikimedia Commons)*